SO-BAU-531

TESTIMONIALS

"Most people have no idea how much money they may lose over the course of their lives by unthinkingly applying for Social Security benefits at the earliest opportunity. This excellent book explains how to thoughtfully decide when to apply, in a language that everybody can easily understand. Anybody considering retirement in the near future could learn a lot—and earn a lot—by reading this book."

Bruce Schobel, FSA, MAAA
Actuary and Former Social Security Administration Advisor

"At Grandparents.com, we empower grandparents with information so they can take care of themselves, as well as their families. Brian Doherty's book *Getting Paid To Wait: Bigger Social Security Benefits—the Simple and Easy Way* is an indispensable resource for people approaching retirement who need to get strategic about one of their most important financial decisions—when to claim their Social Security benefits. Brian's Getting Paid To Wait strategies are straightforward, easy to understand, and can make a huge financial difference in the quality of life many people will enjoy in their retirement. It doesn't matter if you are single, married, divorced, or widowed; before you claim your Social Security benefits, you need to read this book."

Steve Leber
Chairman and CEO, Grandparents.com

"Anyone who reads Brian Doherty's book, *Getting Paid To Wait* will learn some valuable things about our Social Security system they probably never knew. I didn't know there was so many options available when it comes to claiming your Social Security benefits. Doherty cuts through all the clutter and focuses on a few things that almost everybody could use to substantially increase their Social Security income and even get paid to wait while they are doing it. He uses meaningful examples with tables and charts that are easy to understand. *Getting Paid To Wait* is an invaluable resource and a must read for anybody in the process of deciding when to claim their Social Security benefits."

Ed Moslander
Senior Managing Director, TIAA-CREF Head of Institutional Client Services

"A compelling book you won't want to put down until you read every word! *Getting Paid To Wait* caused me to stop and assess my own Social Security strategy as I move through my 60s. Anyone from wage earners to entrepreneurs can benefit from a delayed but calculated strategy in maximizing the most benefits you can receive. This book is especially important for ANY woman who must make Social Security decisions in her future. And with so many people living longer, each section of this book gives new reasons to stop, calculate, then collect. The various examples of salaries, marital status, and claiming benefits from age 62 to age 70 are comprehensive, believable, and persuasive.

I highly recommend this book to anyone who values the importance of their financial future."

Carole Copeland Thomas, MBA, CDMP
Global Diversity Consultant and Trainer

"Brian Doherty has written an important and accessible book on a topic that can make a significant difference in the financial lives of most people. He provides real insights and useful recommendations in a book that is very well written and easy to understand. This book should be required reading for all who are concerned about their financial security and how to maximize their Social Security benefits the simple and easy way."

Mathew Greenwald
President, Mathew Greenwald & Associates

GETTING PAID TO WAIT

ACT NOW!
Special Edition

Bigger Social Security Benefits— The Simple and Easy Way

BY BRIAN DOHERTY

Foreword by Farrell Dolan

ACANTHUS PUBLISHING
BOSTON, MA

Doherty, Brian, 1957-
  Getting paid to wait : bigger Social Security benefits -- the simple and easy way / by Brian Doherty ; foreword by Farrell Dolan.

  pages : illustrations ; cm

  ISBN: 978-0-9972001-0-2

  1. Social security--United States. 2. Older people--United States--Finance, Personal. 3. Retirement income--United States--Planning. I. Dolan, Farrell. II. Title.

HD7125 .D64 2014
368.4/300973

Copyright © 2015, Brian Doherty
All rights reserved.
ISBN: 978-0-9905536-4-9

All rights reserved. No part of this book may be reproduced or transmitted in any form or by any means, electronic or mechanical, including photocopying, recording, or by any information storage and retrieval system, without written permission of the author, except for the inclusion of brief quotations in a review.

Published by Acanthus Publishing, Boston, Massachusetts

PRINTED IN USA
10 9 8 7 6 5 4 3 2 1

The content of this book is intended to be an introduction to some of the Social Security topics that are most likely to play a role in your retirement planning. It is not intended to be a substitute for personalized advice from a professional advisor. The information presented in this book is general and for educational purposes only; it may not apply to your specific circumstances. The material presented may provide clues, but not necessarily answers for your specific situation and is presented with the intent of accuracy based on current law. Please keep in mind that everyone's individual situation is unique. Congress may change the law governing benefit amounts at any time.

Every effort has been made to ensure this publication is as accurate and complete as possible. However, no representations or warranties are made with respect to the accuracy or completeness of the contents of this book. It is not the intent of this publication or its authors to provide professional tax, investment, or legal advice. The strategies contained herein may not be suitable for your situation. You should consult with a professional where appropriate. This publication should be used only as a general guideline and not as the ultimate source of information about Social Security claiming strategies.

The content of this book is intended to be informational and educational and DOES NOT constitute financial advice. We strongly recommend that you seek the advice of a tax, legal, and financial services professional before making decisions related to any investment or other financial decisions. Neither the Publisher nor the Author is responsible for the consequences of any decisions or actions taken in reliance upon or as a result of the information provided in this book.

The text includes information about some of the tax consequences of Social Security benefits. While nothing contained within should be constructed as tax advice, any tax-related information is not intended or written to be used, and cannot be used, for the purpose of avoiding penalties under the Internal Revenue Code or promoting, marketing, or recommending to another party any transaction or matter addressed in this book.

Neither the author nor the Publisher can be held responsible for any direct or incidental loss resulting from applying any of the information provided or incidental loss resulting from applying any of the information provided, or from any other source mentioned. The information provided does not constitute any legal, tax, or accounting advice.

TABLE OF CONTENTS

I WOULD LIKE TO DEDICATE THIS BOOK TO:

My wife, Dorese. Thank you for always believing in me, especially during those times that I didn't even believe in myself.

IMPORTANT NOTICE
SOCIAL SECURITY CHANGES

The Social Security rules and regulations have changed since this book was published in January 2015. On November 2, 2015 the Bipartisan Budget Act of 2015 was signed into law by President Obama. That Act included some major changes to Social Security. The changes involved the elimination of certain claiming strategies, the File and Suspend strategy and the Restricted Application strategy. Both of those strategies are explained and illustrated in this book.

The Restricted Application strategy, which I refer to as the Claim Early, Claim Late strategy, is outlined in detail in Chapter 12. The File and Suspend strategy is outlined in detail in Chapter 13. Both claiming strategies were becoming more popular because using either strategy could potentially pay you up to an additional $90,000 in Social Security income. That is probably one of the main reasons why the Federal Government decided to eliminate the strategies.

But, and this is a big But, you may still be able to use one of these incredible claiming strategies before they are gone forever.

FILE AND SUSPEND – USE IT OR LOSE IT

If you are age 66 before May 1, 2016, you can still use the File and Suspend strategy outlined in Chapter 13, but (another big But) you must actually use or implement the strategy before May 1, 2016. Even if you qualify to use the strategy but don't do so before May 1, 2016, you can never use it. So, use it by May 1, 2016 or lose it.

If you qualify to use this strategy, you should become knowledgeable about how the strategy works (the strategy is explained and illustrated in Chapter 13) because using it could potentially pay you tens of thousands of dollars in additional Social Security income.

RESTRICTED APPLICATION
YOU HAVE MORE TIME TO USE IT

If you are age 62 or older before January 1, 2016, you can still use the Claim Early, Claim Late strategy (Restricted Application) outlined in Chapter 12. The difference with this strategy is you don't have to use it or implement it before that date. As long as you are age 62 or older before January 1, 2016, you are Grandfathered and can still use the strategy after that date.

If you qualify to use this strategy, you should become knowledgeable about how the strategy works (the strategy is explained and illustrated in Chapter 12) because using it could potentially pay you tens of thousands of dollars in additional Social Security income.

You may even qualify to use both strategies and can choose the one that is the best option for your personal situation.

MINIMAL CHANGES TO THE BOOK

The first edition of this book was published in January 2015, before all the recent changes. This is a new, special edition of the book but it is very similar to the first edition with a few changes. I have kept the changes to a minimum because I want the people who are still qualified to use these incredible Social Security claiming strategies, to use them before they are gone forever. You can still get paid while you wait to maximize your Social Security benefits but in order to do so, you may have to ACT NOW!

ACKNOWLEDGEMENTS

Thank you to the love of my life, my wife of over 30 years, Dorese, for her incredible patience and encouragement during the four years that it took me to write this book. Thank you for standing by me through the ups and downs of my career. Thank you for your acceptance of my extensive travel schedule and the great home life that was always waiting for me when I returned. I wouldn't be where I am today without you. Thank you for agreeing to spend the rest of your life with me, for the sacrifices you made in support of my career and our family, and thank you for your unconditional love and support. I love you, Dear.

Thank you to my three children: Caitlin, Matthew, and Shannon. You inspire me to be a better husband, father, and human being. I cherish our close relationship and hope I can always live up to your expectations. I love you more than you know.

Thank you to my mother and father, Frank and Mary Doherty, for my great childhood. Mom, thank you for always being there when Dad was on the road. Dad, thank you for working so hard to provide for your family. Thank you both for giving me the gift of your unconditional love and my Roman Catholic faith, which is the foundation of my life and my source of strength and comfort. Dad, thank you for giving me one of the greatest examples of how to be a great husband and a great father. Thank you both for always encouraging me to be my best and thank you for always being there for me. I love you both dearly.

Thank you to my in-laws, Barb and Dave Lewis. Our friendship has grown deeper and stronger over the years. I truly enjoy the time we spend together; either at our house in up-state New York or your house in Florida. Thank you for your interest in the progress of my book and thank you for your encouragement and support. I love you both.

Thank you to my mentor and friend, Farrell Dolan. Thank you for saying "yes" when I called you almost 10 years ago and asked you if you still wanted to do some stuff in the retirement income space. The three years that we worked together were some of the most productive and happiest times of my career. Your passion for retirement income planning inspired my interest in the topic, which eventually led to my enlightenment of our great Social Security system and its importance in the lives of most retirees in this country. Our time working together has had a profound impact on my life and I feel incredibly fortunate that our paths crossed for that brief period of time. I feel even more fortunate that I can call you "friend".

Thank you to my writing mentor, Sydney LaBlanc. Thank you for your inexhaustible patience and assistance you generously provided during the time I was writing this book. I put great value on the advice and direction you gave me, but the one thing I found to be invaluable during that period of time was your friendship. Sometimes it gets lonely writing a book, and I found our long talks on the telephone to be just the break and inspiration I needed to continue the grind. Your great sense of humor and your ability to make me laugh gave me something else to look forward to other than your great advice on writing.

Thank you to Leo Pusateri for introducing me to Sydney LaBlanc.

Thank you to my other writing mentor and business advisor, Paige Stover. Thank you for editing my book and making it easier to read and understand. Thank you for taking me seriously when I told you I wanted to improve the lives of millions of people by helping them make better Social Security claiming decisions. With your business and marketing advice, along with your team at Ictus Initiative, I have never been more confident that we can help millions of people enjoy a more financially comfortable retirement.

Thank you to my friend, Tom Hegna, for recommending that I work with Paige Stover.

Thank you to George Kasparian and David Kennedy at Ictus Initiative for building my Social Security Calculator, which will be a critical tool for helping people make better Social Security claiming decisions based on the concepts outlined in my book.

Thank you to Ian Nichols and Timesha Livingston for their creative efforts and design work in the production of this book.

Thank you to Kate Tarbell, Zi Benni Zang, Chase Souders, Lily Fisher, and Lois Hager for assisting Paige and me during the editorial process of my book.

Thank you to Ted Mathis, the CEO at New York Life where I worked for 13 incredible years. After listening to Ted give a presentation on the benefits of guaranteed lifetime income, little did I know how it would change my life in so many positive ways. It was Ted Mathis who first made me aware of the financial challenges that so many single women encounter in their retirement years. Thank you, Ted, for putting me on the path that eventually led to me discovering all the benefits of our Social Security system.

Thank you to Bruce Schobel for not only providing most of the longevity statistics for the book, but also for proofreading the book for accuracy.

Thank you to Larry Harvazinski, my tax accountant and CPA, for verifying the accuracy of all the numbers in Chapter 11.

Thank you to all my friends at New York Life, including Andy Reiss, Karen Dann, John Morelli, Al Cohn, Doug Brino, Ed Wilson, Pearse McCormack, Scott Sanders, Mary Roberts, Angela Buro, Jessica Cooke, Dan Shikes, Jerry Combs, Bill Feakes, Matt Malone, Mark Rosky, Bob Rock, John Meyer, Anne Marie Woods, Frank Vilcnik, Rupesh Kotiya, Dave Zimmerman, Cody Phillips, TG Nawn, Mike Kearns, Tim Porter, Steve Rathford, Andrew Williams, Matt Dettman, Matt Domich, Irwin Silber, Russ Clark, Jeff Smith, Marc Whitelaw, Matt Costello, Troy Glover, Andrew Cappaccio, Maryanne Wekow, Melissa Gaustad, Jeremy Smith, Matt Leung, Ran Sarkar, Sheila Erickson, Philip Caminiti, Tracy Corroon Rich Rothenberger, Jose Barros and Steve Long.

FOREWORD

When I met Brian Doherty at a financial services industry meeting in February 2007, my life was moving at the speed of light. As a guest speaker at the conference, I had been billed as an expert, a "pioneer", in the emerging field of retirement income planning. Coincidentally, I had just retired at age 58 from Fidelity Investments after the introduction of the new 'income planning' project was enthusiastically embraced by investors. It was time to practice what I preached. It was time to take the theories I'd been suggesting to people and apply them to my own life. That way, my wife and I could set out into this new stage of life with confidence.

Brian and I spoke at great length during that meeting. It was clear that he believed too many people who were my age, and approaching retirement, did not have much knowledge on how Social Security actually worked. He was convinced that few advisers knew much about Social Security in general. Brian asked a basic question: "With so much at stake, how can anyone make an informed decision concerning Social Security when they don't know the rules and the assortment of claiming options available?" The obvious answer: they can't. I couldn't, either—until I met Brian Doherty. Even I, a purported "expert" in the world of income planning, wasn't quite clear on the rules and idiosyncrasies of Social Security claiming.

My awareness was raised; making a bad decision about when to begin taking Social Security benefits could have a major impact on the amount of income my wife and I received during our retirement years, which were likely to be many. It's not uncommon to see a poor decision result in a diminished income of up to $50,000, or even $100,000, compared to what could be earned. When it came time for me to make my own claiming decision, I knew I couldn't afford a mistake like that.

Researching Social Security, talking to the Social Security Administration to get clarification, and making all that research relevant to my own unique circumstance, was not only time consuming, but—to be honest—pretty boring, too. Luckily, Brian has done the work for us in his book. He talked to the government people, clarified details, and, most importantly, constructed an easy, concise, and understandable way for you and me to understand our options and the wonderful benefits of Social Security. He has outlined strategies that will show you how to best utilize Social Security so that you receive more income throughout your retirement.

The most powerful sources of income during retirement are those that are guaranteed for life and are impervious to market risks and adjust to inflation. There are only two sources of income with this kind of protection: an increasingly rare defined benefit plan (which sometimes do not adjust to inflation), and Social Security. It is imperative that anyone taking the intimidating leap into retirement knows how to take full advantage of the amazing Social Security benefits available.

Brian also caused me to reflect on the impact that the decision to claim Social Security had on my wife and on many other spouses, especially women. So many married couples rush into their claiming decision thinking that they should "take the money and run". They do not pause and think about the fact that, at some point in the future, one of them will be living alone, without the monthly Social Security check that was coming regularly before the death of the first spouse. This book showed me the vital importance of making sure my wife will receive the largest benefit possible if I am the first one to go and statistically, the husband generally predeceases the wife. These issues are so important, but so misunderstood by the people making the decisions.

Thankfully, Brian Doherty has done something about this lack of understanding. He has written a book that makes clear the importance of thoughtful analysis before you claim and gives you a simple and easy framework to evaluate your options. I have spent many years in the financial services industry and I have never seen this issue explained with such precision and clarity. Brian has done a great service for people contemplating retirement, particularly those between age 60 and age 62. I think this book ought to be a standard 60th birthday gift for everyone.

Farrell Dolan
Executive Vice President, Fidelity Investments (Retired)
September 30, 2014

AUTHOR'S INTRODUCTION

I am assuming that you bought this book because you are in the process of making your Social Security claiming decision. Deciding when to claim your Social Security benefits will probably be the most important financial decision of your life. For many years, the conventional wisdom in this country was to claim your Social Security benefits as early as possible, which meant at age 62. For many people, this was not the best decision. If I were to tell you what I really thought, I would say many of those people who have already claimed their benefits at age 62 have made a poor decision. I believe the decision to claim early is frequently made because people are uninformed and they have gone along with conventional wisdom. I didn't write this book for the people who have already claimed their benefits, because this book can't help them. They have already made their decision, and they can't change it. They will have to live with it for the rest of their lives.

You, on the other hand, are in a different position. You haven't decided on a course of action yet and you still have options available and choices to make. All I ask is that, while you are reading this book, you keep an open mind. I wrote this book in order to help you make the best possible Social Security claiming decision for your particular circumstances. For some people, claiming benefits at age 62 may be the best decision. But many others can greatly increase the amount of their Social Security benefits if they educate themselves on the options and become strategic in how they manage their claiming decision.

Recently, there has been a major shift in thinking in this country, and an increasing number of people are deciding to delay claiming their benefits. The percentage of people claiming their Social Security benefits at age 62 has been decreasing over the last 10 years. In fact, in 2012, the percentage of people who claimed their benefits at age 62 was the lowest percentage in almost 30 years. In 2012, 200,000 fewer people claimed their Social Security benefits at age 62 when compared to the number who claimed at that same age just three years earlier, in 2009. Also, in 2012, we saw the largest number of people who waited and claimed their benefits at age 66 in almost 30 years.[1]   There may be several reasons why this is happening, but whatever the reason, it doesn't appear that this trend is going to reverse itself anytime soon; it actually appears to be just the opposite. As the general public becomes more aware of the financial advantages they receive by delaying their benefits, this trend seems to be gaining steam.

The trend is clear, so why are so many people choosing to delay claiming their Social Security benefits? There may be several answers to that question, but it appears that one of the biggest reasons for the delay is that people are realizing how much bigger their monthly Social Security check will be if they delay. They know that the longer they delay claiming their benefits, the larger their monthly check will be and how much easier it will be to pay their bills because of it. This will reduce their financial worries and allow them to live a better quality of life in their retirement. However, it's not just about the bigger monthly check. They may also realize that when they delay claiming their benefits, it puts them in a better position to take full advantage of all the great things Social Security has to offer. These other great things are precisely what this book is about. Once you learn more about the system, it should become clear to you why so many more people are deciding to delay claiming their Social Security benefits.

Therefore, if you shouldn't start taking your benefits at age 62, when should you start?

The answer to this question will probably be the last, great financial decision of your lifetime. I know that sounds very dramatic, but I can almost guarantee you that by the time you finish this book, you will be a believer.

In the course of my career in the financial services industry, I discovered that very few people, even those in the financial services industry, knew very much about Social Security. I spent the last six years of my corporate career focused exclusively on educating financial advisors at some of the largest banks and investment companies in this country on the financial challenges people face in their retirement years.

Most of my 25 years in the financial services industry were spent either directly or indirectly helping individuals accumulate assets and savings so they could retire comfortably. I had always thought that accumulated assets and savings would be the primary source of income for most people in their retirement. I didn't think their Social Security income was going to be substantial or important. Because of this mindset, I knew very little when it came to Social Security because I never gave it much thought. Even after I became educated on the Social Security system, I still resisted the notion of how critically important it is to the majority of people in this country.

As my education continued, the evidence became overwhelming. I came to the conclusion that Social Security income is incredibly important to most people in this country, even for those who retire with a substantial amount of accumulated savings and assets. Shortly after coming to this conclusion, I had an epiphany... I realized that the majority of people in this country get very little guidance when making their Social Security claiming decision. That didn't seem right to me. Most people are making the single most important financial decision of their lifetime with little or no advice or guidance! With that in mind, I decided to write this book.

WHAT'S IN IT FOR YOU?

By delaying the claiming of your Social Security benefits, you increase the size of your benefit. In other words, you increase the dollar amount of the monthly Social Security check you will receive for the rest of your life. In order to maximize the size of your benefit or make your Social Security check as large as possible, you should delay claiming your benefits as long as possible, ideally until age 70. Having said that, I realize that thoughts may be going through your head along the lines of, "If he thinks I'm going to wait until I am 70 years old before I start receiving my Social Security benefits, he's out of his mind. There is no way I am waiting that long before I start receiving checks from Social Security!"

I want you to know, I GET IT! I understand you don't want to wait that long. However, when you learn how you can get paid a substantial amount of Social Security income while you wait, you may change your mind. Let me show you what's in it for you:

> 1.) If you are a married or divorced couple who is 62 or older before January 1, 2016, a widow, or a widowed spouse, you can delay claiming your Social Security benefits, but still receive some income from Social Security while you wait. In other words, while you are deferring your benefit, you can still receive some income, in many cases a substantial amount of money, from Social Security. I know that may sound hard to believe, but it's true.

> 2.) If you are married, after one of you dies, you want to make sure the surviving spouse is left with the biggest monthly

Social Security check possible. You want to leave the survivor in a financial position to enjoy a good quality of life and maintain his or her financial independence. Most married couples actually do the opposite. After the first spouse dies, the surviving spouse is left with the smallest monthly Social Security check possible, which greatly increases the probability that the surviving spouse will struggle financially.

3.) If you are divorced, but were married for at least 10 years, you usually have the same claiming options that married couples do. In fact, Social Security allows divorced spouses to do some things that even married couples can't. Divorced men and women have more Social Security claiming options available to them than single people who were never married, or people who were married for less than 10 years before their divorce.

4.) If you are not married, I will give you some very compelling reasons why you should delay claiming your Social Security benefits as long as possible.

5.) If you have some accumulated savings, there are some incredible tax benefits associated with Social Security income and how you may be able to reduce, or even eliminate, the amount of taxes you pay simply by getting a higher percentage of your retirement income from Social Security.

In the chapters that follow, we will look at several married couples who are in the process of making their claiming decision and use their stories as examples of the choices people should consider as they contemplate the claiming of their Social Security benefits. Then, we will examine the various Why Wait Factors. These are the issues that you need to take into consideration as you weigh the pluses and minuses of deferring your claiming decision.

WHY WAIT FACTORS:

Why Wait Factor #1 – You're Probably Going to Live Longer Than You Think

Why Wait Factor #2 – The Odds That You Will Die Before You Claim Your Benefits Are Very Low

Why Wait Factor #3 – Social Security is Not Going Away Anytime Soon

Why Wait Factor #4 – The Pay Increase Benefit

Why Wait Factor #5 – The Survivor Benefit

Why Wait Factor #6 – Too Many Women Struggle Financially

Why Wait Factor #7 – The Spousal Benefit

Why Wait Factor #8 – The Working Longer Benefit

Why Wait Factor #9 – The Tax Benefit

Later in the book, I will walk you through the Getting Paid To Wait[SM] strategies that make the most sense for qualified married couples—Claim Early, Claim Late (Restricted Application) and File and Suspend. Just like the names imply, these are the claiming strategies in which a married couple can receive some Social Security income while they are delaying the claiming of their benefits. I know this may sound unbelievable, but it's true and every qualified married couple should be aware of these strategies before they make their Social Security claiming decision. Then, finally, we will look at the special circumstances of divorce and delve into special ways that qualified divorced spouses can maximize their Social Security benefits.

Even though more and more people are deciding to delay claiming their benefits every year, many people still make the decision to claim at age 62. I call this the Claim As Early As Possible strategy. If you decide to claim your benefits at age 62, that decision could end up costing you hundreds of thousands of dollars in lost Social Security income over your retirement lifetime. If you use the Claim As Early As Possible strategy, you will also receive the smallest dollar increases possible in the size of your Social Security check every year for the rest of your life. And, if you are married, you will also leave either you or your spouse with the smallest Social Security check possible after the first spouse dies. This book will show you how to make a better decision and increase your Social Security income by tens of thousands of dollars, or in many cases, by hundreds of thousands of dollars, over your retirement lifetime. It will also show you how to get the largest dollar increases in the size of your Social Security check every year for the rest of your life and how you can leave a surviving spouse with the biggest Social Security check possible after the first spouse dies. It's a lot easier than you think.

You will see that the Social Security Administration jumps through hoops and bends over backward to give people in this country every opportunity to maximize their Social Security income. Unfortunately, most people are not aware of these options and, as a result, many end up minimizing their income or getting the smallest check possible. I don't want you to be one of those people. When you finish this book, you should know exactly how to get the most money you can from Social Security in your particular circumstances.

Before you get upset because you think I am going to tell you that you have to work until you are 70 years old, let me assure you, that does not have to be the case. Although, I think it does make a great deal of sense for many people to work a few years longer and take advantage of the seven Wait Factor Bonuses that we will explore in Chapter 10. If you choose not to work longer, I'll show you the incredible Getting Paid To Wait claiming strategies that a qualified married couple, and many qualified divorced spouses, can use that may allow them to retire and still delay claiming their Social Security benefits.

The basic message in this book applies whether you have accumulated savings and assets as you transition into retirement, or if you don't have any savings and your Social Security check is going to be your only source of income in retirement. Either way, the concepts in this book can have a significant impact on improving your quality of life and standard of living in retirement.

At the very least, by the time you finish reading this book, you will no longer be uninformed or uneducated when it comes to the options available for you. You may still decide to claim your Social Security benefits early, even at age 62, but that decision will not be an uninformed one.

SOURCES:

1. Social Security Administration, Annual Statistical Supplement (Washington, DC: SSA, 2013)

BRIAN DOHERTY

PART I

62-70: THE EIGHT MOST IMPORTANT YEARS OF YOUR LIFE

YOUR LAST, GREAT FINANCIAL DECISION

MAKING THE RIGHT DECISION CAN MAKE OR BREAK YOU

Your decision about when to start receiving your Social Security benefits will probably be the last, great financial decision of your lifetime. Unfortunately, many people in this country do not make a good decision when they claim their benefits. Making a good decision about when to begin your Social Security benefits could mean you (and if married, you and your spouse) will receive tens of thousands of dollars of additional income from Social Security during your retirement lifetime. If you live to your full life expectancy or beyond, it could result in Social Security paying you hundreds of thousands of dollars of additional income.

At this point, you also may be thinking, "Come on, does it really make that big of a difference when I start my Social Security benefits?" The answer to that question is—YES. Absolutely, it does. The age at which you decide to start receiving your Social Security checks can make a very big difference in how comfortable you are in your retirement. This will be the case whether you have other money (savings) or don't have any other money and Social Security is going to be your only source of income in your retirement.

For most of you reading this book, your Social Security claiming decision will truly be the most important financial decision you will ever make in your lifetime. This decision can have a dramatic impact on your standard of living and quality of life in retirement—especially in your later years. That's why the eight years from age 62 to age 70 could be the most important years of the rest of your life. If you make a good decision during those years and maximize your Social Security benefits, then you or both you and your spouse will be in a better position to experience a more financially secure retirement.

BIG BENEFIT OF WAITING

Claiming your Social Security benefits, sometimes referred to as your Social Security claiming decision, refers to the age at which you begin to receive your Social Security checks. For example, when I refer to claiming your Social Security benefits at age 62, this means you have notified the Social Security Administration that you want to start receiving your monthly Social Security checks when you reach age 62. The Social Security Administration gives you the option of claiming your benefits at any time between the ages of 62 and 70. Therefore, you could claim your Social Security benefits as early as age 62, you could wait until age 70, or you could claim them anytime between the ages of 62 and 70.

You may be thinking to yourself, "why would anybody wait until age 70 to claim their Social Security benefits when they can begin them eight years earlier at age 62?" The answer is very simple. If you wait until age 70 to claim or begin your Social Security benefits, your monthly check will be approximately 76% larger than the check you will receive if you claim at age 62. For example, Sandy claimed her Social Security benefits at age 62 and her monthly checked totaled $1,000. If she waited and claimed her benefits at age 70, Sandy's monthly Social Security check would increase to $1,760. By waiting until age 70 to claim her benefits, Sandy will receive an additional $760 ($1,760 - $1,000) every month for the rest of her life. You can begin receiving your Social Security benefits at ANY TIME between the ages of 62 and 70. Therefore, if you don't claim them when you are 62 years old, you could claim them when you are 63 years old or wait until you are 64, 65, 66, 67, 68, 69, or 70 years old. Each year that you delay will increase the amount of your monthly Social Security check by a certain set percentage. For every year you delay, you are guaranteed to receive a larger check for the rest of your life.

KEY CONCEPTS

Work History Benefit – Your Social Security Work History Benefit is the benefit that most people are familiar with—the monthly checks you will receive for the rest of your life. The size of your Work History Benefit is determined by the number of years you worked, the amount of money you made, and the amount of Social Security taxes you paid over your entire career, which are usually called payroll taxes or FICA. Usually, the longer you work, the more money you make, and the more payroll taxes you pay over your working life, the larger your Social Security check or Work History Benefit will be when you retire.

The Social Security Administration does not use the term Work History Benefit. In their materials and on their website, they call it your Primary Insurance Amount, or PIA for short. If you go to the Social Security website, they will refer to your Work History Benefit as your Primary Insurance Amount or PIA.[1]

Full Retirement Age – Your Full Retirement Age is very important, and it isn't the same for everybody. Your Social Security Full Retirement Age is determined by the year in which you were born. At one point in time, age 65 was the Full Retirement Age for everyone, regardless of your date of birth. That changed in 1983. You can go to the Social Security website at www.socialsecurity.gov to find out what your Full Retirement Age is, or you can look at reference Table 1.1. It is important to know what your Full Retirement Age is because the amount of money you will receive at your Full Retirement Age is considered your full benefit.

TABLE 1.1

A	B	C	D
Year of Birth	Full Retirement Age	Percentage (%) REDUCTION if Claimed at Age 62	Percentage (%) INCREASE if Claimed at Age 70
1943-1954	66	25.00%	32.00%
1955	66, 2 Months	25.83%	30.67%
1956	66, 4 Months	26.67%	29.33%
1957	66, 6 Months	27.50%	28.00%
1958	66, 8 Months	28.33%	26.67%
1959	66, 10 Months	29.17%	25.33%
1960 and Later	67	30.00%	24.00%

The Social Security Administration's definition of Full Retirement Age has been increasing for a number of years and will continue to increase depending on the year you were born. Currently, only if you were born in (or prior to) 1937, is 65 years old considered your Full Retirement Age. If you were born after 1937, depending on your birth year, your retirement age is older than age 65.

> Throughout this book, I will assume the reader was born after 1937 because most of you who are still making your claiming decision will have been born after that date. I have also assumed the reader was born sometime between 1943 and 1954 and has a Full Retirement Age of age 66. Don't worry if you determine that your Full Retirement Age isn't age 66. The basic concepts will work the same, but your numbers will be slightly different. For clarity and simplicity, I will use the ages 62, 66, and 70 to illustrate the strategies I am suggesting.

Looking at Table 1.1, in column A, find the year in which you were born, then move over to column B—there you will find your Full Retirement Age. If you were born anytime between 1943 and 1954, for example, then your Full Retirement Age is age 66. If you were born after 1954, your Full Retirement Age gradually increases. Anyone born in the year 1960 or later has a Full Retirement Age of 67. Your Full Retirement Age serves as your baseline.

Regardless of your age when you claim your benefit, the size of the monthly Social Security check you receive is going to be determined by the size of your benefit at your Full Retirement Age. If you claim your benefit at your Full Retirement Age, then you will receive 100% of that benefit, or the full amount. If you claim your benefit at any other age, you will receive an amount less than 100% if you claim before your Full Retirement Age, and more than 100% if you defer and claim after your Full Retirement Age.

Assuming your Full Retirement Age is 66, if you claim your Social Security benefit at age 62, Column C in Table 1.1 shows you that your Social Security Full Retirement Age Benefit check will be REDUCED by 25%. Column D shows you that your benefit will be INCREASED by 32% if you wait and claim your benefits at age 70.

In the past, typically a few months before your birthday, you received a statement in the mail from Social Security that showed what your Estimated Benefits will be when you retire. A few years ago, Social Security stopped sending those statements out in the regular mail. Recently, however, they changed their mind and decided to send the statements again, but only every five years instead of every year. You can also go to Social Security's website and view the statement of your benefits online. On your statement, it shows you the amount of your estimated benefits at three different ages—at age 62, at age 66, your assumed Full Retirement Age, and at age 70.

CASE STUDY: SANDY ANALYZES THE TIMING OF HER CLAIM

Sandy's Social Security Work History Benefit at her Full Retirement Age of 66 will be $1,000 per month. If she waits until she is 66 years old to claim her Social Security benefits, she will receive that full amount or a monthly check of $1,000. However, if she decides that she doesn't want to wait until she is 66 years old and wants to claim early at age 62, the amount she will receive every month is going to be reduced, in this case, by 25%. Therefore, instead of receiving $1,000 per month at age 66, she is only going to receive $750 per month because she claimed her benefits early at age 62. She will receive this reduced Social Security benefit for the rest of her life.

TABLE 1.2

$1,000 x .25 = $250
$1,000 - $250 = $750 (size of check at age 62)

Most likely, the size of your Social Security check will be different from the numbers in the Sandy example. What won't be different is the size of the percentage reduction. For everybody who claims their Social Security benefits at age 62, the amount of the reduction will be 25%.

If you receive a monthly Social Security check of $750, multiply the monthly check amount by 12 to determine your annual benefit. In this case, Sandy would receive a total of $9,000 of Social Security income for the year ($750 x 12 = $9,000). By claiming benefits earlier, at age 62, Sandy only receives $9,000 for the year, instead of the $12,000 ($1,000 x 12) she would have received by claiming at age 66, her Full Retirement Age.

The opposite happens if Sandy delays claiming her benefits past her Full Retirement Age of 66. For every year she delays beyond age 66, she will earn what Social Security calls Delayed Retirement Credits. The size of her monthly Social Security check will increase by 8% for every year that she delays. If she delays claiming her benefits until age 70—four years past her Full Retirement Age of 66—the amount of her monthly Social Security check is going to be 32% (8% x 4) larger, or in this case, $1,320 per month.

TABLE 1.3

$1,000 x .32 = $320
$1,000 + $320 = $1,320 (size of check at age 70)

TABLE 1.4

Age	Monthly Check	Annual Income
62	$750	$9,000
66	$1,000	$12,000
70	$1,320	$15,840

Table 1.4 clearly shows the advantages to delaying. The longer you delay, the larger the monthly Social Security check will be, and the more annual Social Security income you will receive. By waiting to claim at age 70 instead of at age 62, Sandy receives Social Security income of $15,840 every year instead of only $9,000.

THE REASONS WHY PEOPLE CLAIM EARLY

I don't think claiming your benefits at age 62 is always a bad decision. In fact, for a married couple, it often makes more sense for the lower-earning spouse, or the spouse with the smaller Social Security check, to claim his or her benefits at age 62. I don't believe that everybody who claims their Social Security at age 62 has made a bad decision. I also know that some people have no choice and must claim as early as possible.

Through my experience, I've concluded that there are five basic reasons why people claim their Social Security benefits at age 62:

Reason #1: You're broke: "I was laid off from my job in my late 50s (or early 60s) and I haven't been able to find another job. In fact, I've given up trying. I need to claim my Social Security benefits as soon as I can because I desperately need income."

Reason #2: You hate your job: "I hate my job and can't stomach working there for any longer than I have to. As soon as I can claim Social Security benefits, I'm retiring from my job."

Reason #3: You think Social Security is going to disappear: "I am always reading about the funding problems that our Social Security system is going to encounter in the future. It's to the point that I don't think the system is going to survive. The smart thing to do is claim my benefits as soon as possible because who knows how long Social Security is going to be around."

Reason #4: You fear that you will not break even: "If I delay claiming my Social Security benefits until after age 62, say, until age 66 or even age 70, I know my monthly check will be larger, but I will give up years of Social Security income and will not break even until I am in my late 70s, or even older. I don't think I am going to live that long and if I die before my break even age, I would have received more total Social Security income if I had claimed my benefits at age 62."

Reason #5: You fear that you will have an early demise: "I may die before I reach age 66 or age 70 and end up getting nothing from Social Security. After all those years of working and paying Social Security taxes, I am not going to risk getting nothing in return. I am going to claim my Social Security benefits at age 62 and ensure that I at least get something."

I am not going to dispute that Reason #1 and Reason #2 are good reasons to claim early, but I will dispute the other three reasons. We are going to address Reason #3, Reason #4, and Reason #5 later in the book.

MARSHMALLOWS—THE REAL REASON WHY PEOPLE DON'T WANT TO WAIT

The real reason why so many people claim their Social Security benefits early has a lot to do with marshmallows. You may be asking, "How could marshmallows have anything to do with it?" Most people claim their Social Security benefits early because they don't want to wait the additional years before they start receiving their checks! As it turns out, the reason has more to do with basic human behavior than conventional wisdom. This is where the marshmallows come into play!

Basically, people believe that it does not pay to wait, at least not in the short run. They would love to have the larger Social Security check, but they don't want to wait all of those years to get it. They want their check now! It may make sense in the long run, but there is too much uncertainty in the long run and, like the famous English economist John Maynard Keynes said, "In the long run, we're all dead!" Therefore, people reason that they should get their money now and enjoy it while they can, even if it means significantly less money, because it really doesn't pay to wait.

THE EXPERIMENT

In the late 1960s, Walter Mischel, a professor at Stanford University, conducted an experiment with four-year-old children.[2] They would bring one of the 4-year-olds into a room where there was a table, a chair, and a marshmallow sitting on the table. The 4-year-old child was seated at the table and was told that he or she could eat the marshmallow at any time, but if they waited for 15 minutes before they ate it, then they would be given another marshmallow. The child was left alone in the room with a bell. If they rang the bell, the scientist would come back into the room immediately and the child could eat the first marshmallow, but had to forfeit the second one.[3]

Most of the children did not wait the 15 minutes to eat the marshmallow. The average wait time before the majority of the children rang the bell was only three minutes. Their desire to experience the pleasure of eating the one marshmallow was greater than their patience. They would rather have only one marshmallow, almost immediately, rather than delay the pleasurable experience in order to enjoy even more in the future. In other words, they placed a much higher value on having a smaller amount of the pleasurable item (one marshmallow) now, and a much lower value on having a larger amount of the pleasurable item (two marshmallows) sometime in the future. The children didn't think it paid to wait.

The marshmallow experiment with children led to experiments with adults. The marshmallow, or pleasurable item, for adults, was money. When the experiments were conducted with adults, the marshmallow was replaced with money. Similar to the marshmallow experiment with 4-year-old children, the adults were offered a smaller amount of money immediately, or a larger amount of money sometime in the future. The majority of adults chose the smaller amount of money immediately.[4] There were a number of similar experiments done with adults and money and they each had very similar results that led to the same basic conclusion.[5]

Adults place a very high value on having money now, and a much lower value on getting more money, sometimes a lot more money, in the future. Just like the children and the marshmallows, adults are willing to accept less of a pleasurable item, as long as they get it immediately. Adults and children alike want instant gratification. The adults didn't think it paid to wait either.

PREPROPERATION

The term for this type of basic human behavior is preproperation. I first came across the word preproperation when I read the book "Wait: The Art and Science of Delay" by Frank Partnoy.[6] In his book, Mr Partnoy, defines preproperation as the term for acting when we should wait. In other words, to do things right away or immediately when it may be in our best interest to wait and do them later.

Because of preproperation, most people are willing to accept a smaller amount of money now, instead of waiting to receive a substantially larger amount of money in the future. We see a great example of this basic, but powerful, human behavior with lottery winners. A $100 million lottery jackpot is an enormous amount of money to win, which may be paid to the winner in increments of $5 million a year over a period of 20 years. Lottery winners are also given the option of receiving a reduced sum of money immediately. The jackpot amount is usually reduced to about half of the original winnings if they take the lump sum payment immediately. For example, the winnings are reduced to $50 million for the immediate payout. So, the winner has the choice of receiving $100 million over 20 years, or $50 million immediately. The majority of lottery jackpot winners actually take the reduced lump sum immediately, in this case, the $50 million. There may be all kinds of different reasons to justify taking a lesser amount immediately, but they are not the real reasons. The real reason is this incredibly powerful human behavior called preproperation.

Similarly, people who claim their Social Security benefits early may also use several reasons to justify accepting a lot less Social Security income now, instead of waiting and getting a larger amount of Social Security income later. However, the real reason they claim early is preproperation.

Preproperation is the real reason why many people don't think it pays to wait. The main goal of this book is to show you how, when it comes to claiming your Social Security benefits, you can get paid to wait. The Getting Paid To Wait strategies will overcome this powerful human behavior of preproperation and make it easier for you to make a much better Social Security claiming decision.

YOU WILL LIVE WITH YOUR DECISION
FOR THE REST OF YOUR LIFE

Once you make your Social Security claiming decision, you generally can't change it. You will have to live with it for the rest of your life (actually you have up to one year to change your mind, but you will be required to pay back any Social Security income you received). By reading this book, you are giving that decision the careful consideration it deserves. This book will show you how to get the most out of your Social Security benefits and how to MAXIMIZE your Social Security income. With this knowledge, you should be in a position to make a much better Social Security claiming decision and on your way to enjoying a much more comfortable retirement.

CHAPTER 1 IMPORTANT CONCEPTS:

• Making a good decision about when to begin your Social Security benefits could mean you (and if married, you and your spouse) will receive tens of thousands of dollars, or even hundreds of thousands of dollars, of additional income from Social Security during your retirement lifetime.

• The longer you delay the claiming of Social Security, the larger the monthly Social Security check will be, and the more annual Social Security income you will receive.

• **The real reason many people claim their Social Security benefits early is because they don't think it pays to wait.**

• **The Getting Paid To Wait strategies** will show qualified married couples, and divorced and widowed spouses, the Social Security claiming strategy that will pay them the most Social Security income while they delay claiming their benefits.

SOURCES:

1. Social Security Administration, Fast Facts And Figures About Social Security, 2013 (Washington, DC: SSA, August, 2013)

2. Mischel, W. (n.d.). *The Marshmallow Test: Mastering Self-Control.*

3. Lehrer, Jonah, *DON'T!* (New York, New York: The New Yorker, May 8, 2009)

4. Thaler, Richard, *Some Empirical Evidence of Dynamic Inconsistency*, (Ithaca, NY: Cornell University, 1981)

5. George Ainslie, *Breakdown of Will* (United States: Cambridge University Press, 2001).

6. Partnoy, F. (n.d.). *Wait.*

THE HIGHER-EARNING SPOUSE AND THE LOWER-EARNING SPOUSE

Qualified married couples have some amazing Social Security options available to them. It is very important that both spouses know what those options are so they make a Social Security claiming decision that maximizes their benefits. Using the right Getting Paid To Wait claiming strategy can help a qualified married couple receive a much higher amount of Social Security income that they can enjoy while they are both alive. Once the claiming decision is made, the couple will have to live with it for the rest of their lives. (After making your claiming decision, you do have up to one year to change your mind. However, you will be required to pay back any Social Security income you received).

The Getting Paid To Wait strategies can also play a critical role in the wife's ability to maintain her lifestyle and her financial independence after her husband dies. If you are a married man, you will soon learn that your wife is probably going to live longer than you do and that your Social Security claiming decision will probably be the most important financial decision you will make during your wife's lifetime. You read that correctly—for most married couples, the husband's Social Security claiming decision is the most important financial decision made during the wife's lifetime.

SOCIAL SECURITY—AN IMPORTANT ISSUE FOR WOMEN

Wives generally outlive their husbands.[1] Statistically, the wife is most often the lower-earning spouse—at least among the age group of people currently contemplating their claiming decision—and she will have to live with the claiming decision longer than the husband because she will probably outlive him and be left with only the Social Security Survivor Benefit.

Based on the current statistics provided by the Social Security Administration, women are more often than not the recipients of the smaller Social Security check when compared with their male counterparts. According to the Social Security Administration's March 2014 Fact Sheet, "Social Security is Important to Women," women have a longer life expectancy than men and therefore live longer in retirement. This fact sheet also states that in 2012, the average annual Social Security income received by women age 65 and older was $12,520 as opposed to $16,398 for men of the same age.

Making the right Social Security claiming decision can have a significant impact on the degree to which a woman struggles, if at all, after her husband dies. (See more about Social Security as a woman's issue in Chapter 8). When the Getting Paid To Wait strategies are properly executed, you can help prevent a potentially disastrous outcome for the surviving spouse after the first spouse dies.

DETERMINING THE STARTING POINT—YOUR WORK HISTORY BENEFIT

The Getting Paid To Wait strategies are most applicable for qualified married couples who are seeking to maximize the amount they receive from Social Security. For each married couple, there is typically a higher-earning spouse and a lower-earning spouse. In order to maximize your Social Security income, you first need to determine the size of the monthly Social Security check, or your Work History Benefit, at your Full Retirement Age. To determine the amount of your Work History Benefit, visit www.socialsecurity.gov or review your most recent Social Security benefit statement that has been sent to you in the mail. Once both spouses know the amount of their Work History Benefit, it will be easier to make choices, clarify objectives, and select appropriate strategies that will enable you, as a couple, to get the most out of Social Security.

HIGHER-EARNING AND LOWER-EARNING SPOUSES

Identifying the higher-earning and lower-earning spouses within a marriage is of significant importance to making better Social Security claiming decisions. We will be revisiting several example couples, throughout this book in order to illustrate strategic alternatives and make suggestions as to the best way to maximize the couple's income from Social Security. Making a better claiming decision could result in both spouses enjoying a higher amount of Social Security income while they are both alive, but also provide the surviving spouse with a larger Survivor Benefit after the first spouse dies. Because most wives outlive their husbands and usually have the smaller benefit, it is important to understand the effect that Social Security claiming choices have on women. Their financial positions in retirement must be acknowledged and acted upon wisely in order to make a positive reduction in the number of women who struggle financially or even live in poverty!

As we explore the different Social Security claiming options, we will look at the issues from the perspective of Cris and Lee, both 62 years old. We will look at their individual circumstances and evaluate the various factors they should consider. For purposes of the case studies we use in this book, I have assumed Cris is the higher-earning spouse and therefore has the potential to receive the larger Work History Benefit monthly check. Lee is the lower-earning spouse and therefore will be receiving the smaller monthly benefit check. Once Cris and Lee have obtained the amounts of their Work History Benefits, they are prepared to make choices.

DELAYING THE CLAIM OF THE HIGHER-EARNING SPOUSE

The primary goal of the Getting Paid To Wait strategies is to maximize the size of the higher-earning spouse's Social Security benefit. The benefit of the spouse who earned more money over his or her working career—the one who is going to receive the larger check from Social Security—is the benefit you want to delay claiming as long as possible. This will allow you to maximize the size of that check, since it continues to grow in size the longer you delay claiming it. The secondary goal is to allow the married couple to be paid a significant amount of Social Security income while the spouse with the larger benefit delays claiming. While the higher-earning spouse delays, he or she will receive some income, often a significant amount of income, from Social Security while they delay or wait.

In the example, Cris, who will receive the larger Social Security benefit, should delay the claiming of his benefit as long as possible, while Lee, who will receive the smaller benefit, should probably claim as early as possible. The smaller monthly benefit, or Lee's check, will be paid only while both spouses are still living. When one spouse passes away, Lee's smaller check will stop and Cris's larger check will continue, either in the form of a Survivor Benefit or by maintaining Cris's Work History Benefit, if Lee dies first.

With Lee claiming benefits first, it becomes easier for Cris to delay claiming the larger benefit, ideally until age 70. Prior to Cris's claiming, the married couple does receive some Social Security income from Lee's benefit, which is claimed at age 62. The married couple can use their secret weapon, the Spousal Benefit, to receive even more Social Security income while Cris delays (see Chapter 9). By waiting until age 70 to claim a Work History Benefit, Cris also received eight years of Retroactive COLA Credits (see Chapter 6), making his benefit or monthly check even bigger. Cris also maximized the size of the Survivor Benefit (see Chapter 7). This will provide both Lee and Cris with a much larger amount of guaranteed lifetime income or longevity insurance, which provides a higher degree of financial protection against living a long time in retirement (see Chapter 3).

WHAT FOLLOWS ...

In Part II of the book, we will break all of this down and individually examine each of the Why Wait Factors—there are nine of them. In addition to married couples, a number of these Why Wait Factors also apply to unmarried or single individuals. Nine good reasons why you want to give serious consideration to delaying your claim for Social Security benefits. The bottom line, however, is that you really can get paid to wait.

CHAPTER 2 IMPORTANT CONCEPTS:

• The primary goal of the Getting Paid To Wait strategies is to maximize the size of the higher-earning spouse's Social Security benefit. The secondary goal is to pay the couple the most amount of Social Security income while they wait.

• It is very important that both spouses know what their options are so they make a Social Security claiming decision that maximizes their benefits. Once the claiming decision is made, the couple will basically have to live with it for the rest of their lives.

• The Silent Crisis: Many women over age 65 struggle after their husbands pass away.

• Making a better Social Security claiming decision could make a big difference in decreasing the chances that the surviving spouse will struggle financially after the first spouse dies.

SOURCES:

1. Social Security Administration, Social Security Is Important to Women (Washington, DC: SSA, March 2014)

PART II
THE WHY
WAIT
FACTORS

WHY WAIT FACTOR #1 YOU'RE PROBABLY GOING TO LIVE LONGER THAN YOU THINK

They say in real estate that there are three things that are the most important in determining the value of property: location, location, location. When it comes to retirement income planning, it is all about longevity, longevity, longevity.

A very famous person is often credited with having said: "If I knew I was going to live this long, I'd have taken better care of myself." Later, I will reveal the name of this famous person and why you should consider what he said about living a long time before you make your Social Security claiming decision.

THE GENERAL POPULATION AND LIFE EXPECTANCY

Before we look at the longevity statistics for the general population in the United States, we need to define a term we are all familiar with and have heard many times—**life expectancy**. If you are like most people in this country, you may think you have a general idea of what life expectancy means. You have probably heard that life expectancy is increasing in the United States. According to the National Center for Health Statistics' National Vital Statistics Reports, the life expectancy for a man is around 75 years.

Women tend to live longer than men and their life expectancy is around 80 years. Looking at this data, you may think that most men die around age 75 and very few men live beyond that age. Surprisingly enough, that is not the case.

TABLE 3.1

THE SURPRISING REALITY OF LIFE EXPECTANCY

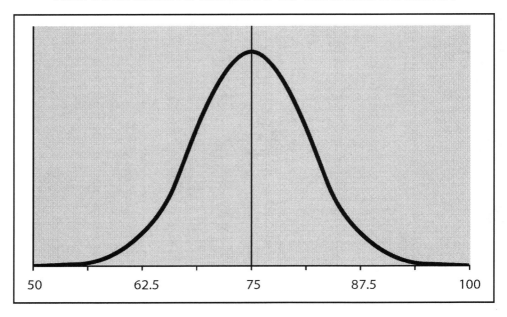

| 50 | 62.5 | 75 | 87.5 | 100 |

LIFE EXPECTANCY IS A MEAN AVERAGE;
APPROXIMATELY 50% DIE BEFORE THAT AGE AND
50% LIVE BEYOND THAT AGE

I was very surprised to learn the true definition of life expectancy. Life expectancy is actually an average; more specifically, a **mean average**. Table 3.1 tells us that approximately 50% of all men die before age 75 and 50% of all men live beyond age 75. That's a lot of men living beyond their life expectancy. I had no idea that such a high percentage (50%) of men lived beyond their life expectancy of 75 years. The numbers are even more shocking for women. If their life expectancy is 80 years, that means that 50% of all women live beyond age 80. That's why longevity is a bigger challenge for women than men.

TABLE 3.2

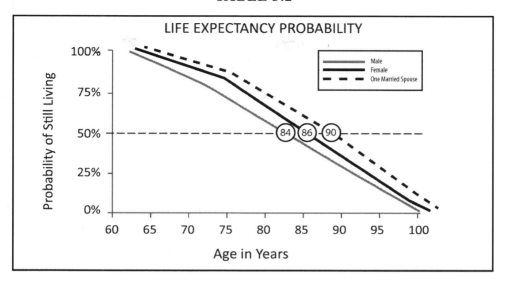

THE LONGER YOU LIVE, THE GREATER YOUR LIFE EXPECTANCY BECOMES.

There is a second aspect to the definition of life expectancy that most people are not aware of. Most people don't know that the longer they live, the farther out they push their life expectancy. You can clearly see that in Table 3.2. If a healthy man reaches age 62, his life expectancy increases from age 75 to age 84.[1] The life expectancy for a woman who reaches age 62 increases from age 80 to age 86. You can see these numbers in Table 3.2.

Healthy men reaching age 62 have a 50% probability of living up to and beyond age 84, and healthy women reaching age 62 have a 50% probability of living up to and beyond age 86.

If you are married, you should plan for the possibility of at least one of you living beyond your life expectancy. If you look at the dotted line in Table 3.2, you can see that the number 90 is circled at the 50% probability. That means, for a married, healthy 62-year-old couple, there is approximately a 50% chance that at least one spouse will live until age 90.

IS IT IN THE GENES?

Many people in this country believe that people are generally living longer; however, they do not think that they will be one of them. Despite all my compelling statistics about the general population of this country living longer, you may still think you are not going to be one of them. After all, you may have had a parent or grandparent who died at a relatively young age in retirement, say, in their 60s or early 70s. You may not think that you are going to live that long because your parent(s) or grandparent(s) didn't and you have their genes. They weren't blessed with the longevity gene, so you figure you weren't either.

PLAN FOR THE POSSIBILITY THAT YOU ARE GOING TO LIVE LONGER THAN YOU THINK.

There has been quite a bit of scientific research conducted to determine how genetics affect longevity. According to Dr. Mark Stibich's article, "The Genetic Theory of Aging," your parents and their genes have about a 35% impact on how long you live.[2] According to research recently published by the University of Gothenburg, exercise, eating right, and medical care, or in other words, how you take care of yourself, have the largest impact on your life expectancy.[3] Your lifestyle has a much bigger impact on your life expectancy than genetics. We know a great deal more about the right kind of lifestyle than our parents did only one generation ago. We benefit from medical advances, new drugs, medical procedures, and equipment that were not around when your parents and grandparents were alive. In fact, even if you don't have the healthiest lifestyle, because of these great medical advances, it is highly likely that you will live longer than your parents did and longer than you expect.

I SPEAK FROM PERSONAL EXPERIENCE

I am fortunate in that, at 57 years old, both of my parents are still alive. My father is 86 years old and my mother is 85 years old. My father's father, my grandfather, died when he was 73 years old of congestive heart failure. My father survived prostate cancer at age 67 and triple bypass heart surgery at age 81. Now, at age 86, he is in great health and he is still working. He loves his job. He says it keeps him young.

My wife of 30 years, Dorese, was diagnosed with breast cancer in her late 40s. Her paternal aunt died of breast cancer in her 20s, and her grandmother died of breast cancer in her mid-50s. Dorese had the cancer removed, underwent radiation treatment, and took a drug for five years to reduce the risk of a recurrence. It has been more than five years since the cancer was discovered, and, at 56, she looks like she is in her late 30s or early 40s. She runs, does yoga, weighs less than she did in high school, and has the healthiest eating habits of anyone I have ever seen.

Five years ago, I found out that I had prostate cancer. I had always thought that eventually I would develop this disease, because my father had it at age 67. I just didn't think I would get it at age 52. A few months after diagnosis, I had my cancerous prostate removed by a robotic surgical device that didn't even exist when my father had his prostate removed. My doctor tells me I am cured and should expect to live a long time.

YOU AND MICKEY MANTLE

My point is this: how long your parents or grandparents lived does have some impact on your life expectancy, but it is a smaller impact than you think. A healthy lifestyle, including regular medical check-ups, which will allow you to discover and quickly treat medical issues, can help extend your life for a very long time.

The famous person I referenced at the beginning of this chapter, who is often credited with having said, "If I knew I was going to live this long, I'd have taken better care of myself," is the Hall of Fame baseball player, Mickey Mantle. Apparently, both his father and grandfather died in their 40s, so he didn't think he was going to live very long either. Mickey Mantle ended up living into his 60s, and it appears that he believed that if he had lived a healthier lifestyle, he may have lived even longer.

Chances are good that you are going to live longer than you think. If you do live longer than you anticipate, you may find yourself saying something similar to what Mickey Mantle said. You may end up saying, "If I knew I was going to live this long, I would have made a different Social Security claiming decision. Instead of claiming my benefits at age 62, I would have delayed at least until age 66, if not longer." The problem is, by the time you come to this realization, it will be too late to do anything about it.

LONGEVITY IS THE #1 THREAT
TO RETIREMENT SECURITY

Living a long time is a wonderful thing. However, from a purely financial perspective, longevity makes it a challenge to maintain your quality of life and your standard of living as you age. Most of us want to be able to maintain our lifestyle for as long as we live. Statistics show that if you've made it this far, you are probably going to be around quite a bit longer. In order to make sure your income will be adequate to meet your basic living expenses, you need to plan ahead, working from the assumption that your life expectancy is probably longer than you think. Just look at the people around you—your aunts and uncles, your neighbors, or the people in your religious or community organization. Many of them are enjoying happy, active lives well into their 80s, some into their 90s. The challenge is to make sure your income will last as long as you do.

RETIREMENT SECURITY AND THE THREAT MAGNIFIERS

In addition to longevity, there are several other potential threats that can put your quality of life at risk. None of these other threats are as daunting or challenging as the risk of living a long time and running out of money. The statistical reality, however, is that the longer you live, the greater the probability is that one of these other threats will materialize and impact your retirement security. If you live for 20, 25, or 30 years in retirement, all of these other threats are intensified and become much more difficult to manage, especially if you have not planned well.

THESE ARE THE FIVE MAJOR THREATS TO YOUR
RETIREMENT INCOME AND YOUR QUALITY OF LIFE:

- Longevity
- Inflation
- Unplanned medical expenses
- Investment ups and downs
- Withdrawing too much, too soon from your savings (2much2soon)

While some of these may be hazardous to your retirement savings, all are potentially hazardous to your retirement income. Longevity is the **threat**

magnifier because it has the potential to magnify, or intensify the risks associated with inflation, healthcare, market volatility, and withdrawal rates.

HOW INFLATION IS AFFECTED BY LONGEVITY

You are probably familiar with the concept of inflation. The term inflation usually refers to increasing prices for goods and services. It is also often referred to as the rate of inflation and is stated in terms of a percentage. For example, you may have read or heard on the news that the annual rate of inflation for a particular year was 2%. This means that, on average, prices rose by 2% during that particular year. Over the last 75 years, the average annual rate of inflation has been somewhere around 3%, based on data provided by the Bureau of Labor Statistics. In all the examples and charts I use in this book, I assume an inflation rate of 3%. Think about the price of a gallon of gas, the price tag on a new car, the cost of a postage stamp, the cost of a new home, and the cost of food. All have increased during the last 10 years. However, the costs of other things, like your cell phone bill and the price of a laptop have come down. So, the average rate of inflation is about 3%.

In most years, the price of goods and services will go up. It is much easier to manage these price increases over shorter periods of time, say 5–10 years. If you live for 20, 25, or 30 years in retirement, it becomes more difficult to incorporate these price increases into your budget and, consequently, longevity becomes the threat magnifier.

TABLE 3.3

Years	0 Yrs	5 Yrs	10 Yrs	20 Yrs	24 Yrs
Percentage (%) Increase	0 %	16 %	34 %	80 %	100 %
Dollar ($) Price	$100	$116	$134	$180	$200

The numbers in Table 3.3 illustrate the effects that a 3% rate of inflation has on the price of a $100 item over different periods of time. The numbers at the top of the table represent the number of years that have gone by. The number 0 Yrs is the starting point, or today. The second line of numbers represents the cumulative total percentage increase in price after the corresponding period of time, and the last line of numbers shows how much the price of that $100 item has increased after those same periods of time.

Table 3.3 shows how difficult it becomes for a retiree to pay for a $100 item over longer periods of time, with an annual inflation rate of only 3%. An item that costs $100 today (0 Yrs) will cost 16% more, or $116 after just five years of inflation. After 10 years of inflation, that same item would cost 34% more, or $134. If you have to pay for this item, you are probably not happy about a 16% price increase over five years, or a 34% price increase over 10 years, but those price increases are still manageable. However, after 20 years, the price increases by 80% and costs $180, and after 24 years, the price doubles, or increases by 100% and costs $200. If we were to go out even farther, say 25 or 30 years, the price increases would get even larger.

You can see how difficult it becomes for retirees to pay all their bills in an inflationary environment. If you live for 20, 25, or even 30 years in retirement, inflation ends up being a big issue because it becomes difficult to pay for these items, especially if you are living on a fixed income. The term fixed income means that a retiree's income remains constant, or fixed, over time. Some of the items that are affected by inflation may be essential things you cannot do without, and it becomes increasingly challenging to make ends meet.

Inflation is a concern whether you are retired or not, but may be easier to manage while you are still working. If you are receiving a salary or an hourly wage and perhaps a pay increase during the course of a year, this can help you keep up with inflation. However, for most retirees, their income is relatively fixed, which makes it difficult to keep up with inflation.

Just looking at the inflation issue, you get a good idea of the challenges that longevity presents to the average retiree. The price of healthcare is increasing at an alarming rate, greater than the general rate of inflation. The other potential threats or risks—market risk and withdrawal rate risk—are a little more complicated and apply to people who have investments and accumulated savings. Longevity, or the threat magnifier, causes each additional threat to become more difficult to manage. However, if you're thinking of investing your assets in bonds or mutual funds as a hedge against inflation, other problems may interfere, such as bear markets. Bear markets (defined as a period where the market goes down 20% or more from peak to trough) can eat away at the stock or stock mutual fund portion of your retirement portfolio in a short time. Even if you are not bitten by a bear market, when you invest your money in stocks or stock mutual funds, your income will depend on stock performance, which tends to be volatile.

IS THERE SUCH A THING AS LONGEVITY INSURANCE?

It would be great if you could get insurance coverage that would protect you against the risk of living too long or, in other words, longevity insurance. You may be surprised to know that you can. You can purchase a longevity insurance policy from some insurance companies, but it is expensive coverage. There is an easier and more practical way—and, for many people, the only way—to get longevity insurance. Before I tell you how you can get longevity insurance, let's briefly discuss the concept of insurance in general.

HOW DOES INSURANCE WORK?

You have most likely purchased some form of insurance in your lifetime—insurance for your car, home, health, or life. You buy insurance for these items or possessions because the cost to fix or replace them could be very high and, consequently, difficult to comfortably assimilate into your monthly or annual budget. Without insurance, most people wouldn't be able to replace their car or home if either was destroyed. Without health insurance, most people wouldn't be able to pay for health care emergencies—an illness requiring major surgery, for example. Without life insurance, in the event of the death of the higher-earning spouse, a young, growing family may not be able to replace the income that the spouse provided, which then creates a financial hardship. The chance of any one of these events happening may be small, but the negative consequences of such an event happening could be catastrophic.

When you purchase insurance for any one of these scenarios, in essence, you transfer the financial risk from any of these events occurring to a much bigger organization, such as an insurance company. If your house burns down and you have homeowner's insurance, the $200,000 cost to replace it will be covered by the insurance company under the terms of your policy. When you buy insurance of any kind, you are simply transferring the risk of loss from yourself to the insurance company. Insurance companies are set up to manage these risks and are structured to absorb the impact of the event and cover the expenses related to the loss.

How can you get longevity insurance that will insure you and your spouse against the risk of living too long and what exactly does longevity insurance do for you? Longevity insurance pays you a guaranteed income for the rest of your life, no matter how long you live. The more longevity insurance you have, the higher the amount of income you will receive for the rest of your life. In other words, it does not matter how long you live, you are guaranteed to receive this income until the day you die.

THE LIFE (STYLE) PRESERVER

There are essentially two ways to acquire longevity insurance:

1. Purchase a longevity insurance policy from an insurance company

2. Delay the claiming of your Social Security benefits as long as possible, allowing you to receive a higher amount of monthly income from Social Security that you are guaranteed to receive for the rest of your life.

Social Security is a form of longevity insurance. Delaying your Social Security benefits as long as possible provides you with a larger amount of longevity insurance than if you claim early. The longer you delay claiming your Social Security benefits, the more longevity risk you transfer from yourself to the federal government. The federal government is in a much better position to manage longevity risk than individual citizens are. When you delay claiming your Social Security benefits, you are actually purchasing longevity insurance in the form of a bigger monthly benefit. This will allow you to receive more income, guaranteed for the rest of your life and possibly for the rest of your spouse's life as well. More guaranteed lifetime income from Social Security reduces the impact of most of the five threats we discussed earlier, and should make your retirement less stressful and more enjoyable. Social Security is a life preserver for your retirement income!

CHAPTER 3 IMPORTANT CONCEPTS:

• Longevity is the first thing you should consider before making your Social Security claiming decision.

• There is a relatively high probability that you could live a long time in retirement, probably longer than you think.

• If you are married, the probability is even higher that at least one of you is going to live a long time. That should be a major consideration when making your Social Security claiming decisions.

• Longevity is actually a threat magnifier. By making the right Social Security claiming decision, you acquire a retirement income life (style) preserver, which should help to preserve your quality of life and standard of living, no matter how long you live.

SOURCES:

1. Official Social Security Website, Retirement & Survivors Benefits: Life Expectancy Calculator (Baltimore, Maryland: SSA, 2014)

2. Stibich, Mark, *The Genetic Theory of Aging* (United States: About.com, May 21, 2014)

3. University of Gothenburg, *Lifestyle Affects Life Expectancy More Than Genetics* (Gothenburg, Sweden: The Sahlgrenska Academy, January 27, 2011)

WHY WAIT FACTOR #2
THE ODDS THAT YOU WILL DIE
BEFORE YOU CLAIM YOUR BENEFITS
ARE VERY LOW

"What if I delay claiming and die before I start to collect my Social Security benefits?" I hear this question a lot. Many people use this as a reason to claim their Social Security benefits at age 62. They worry that if they delay claiming their Social Security benefits until age 66 or age 70, they may die prematurely and then they will get nothing. After all those years of paying Social Security payroll taxes, they feel like they should get something. So to avoid the possibility of getting nothing, they claim their Social Security benefits at age 62. That way, if they die before age 66 or age 70, at least they collected some money from Social Security, even if it was only for a couple of years.

The logic makes sense if you are single and in poor health. But if you are in relatively good health or if you are married and in good or bad health, it doesn't make much sense for two very compelling reasons:

> 1. The first reason is the longevity factor and the probability of living beyond the ages of 66 or 70.

2. The second reason concerns the Survivor Benefit and how it works when a spouse dies before claiming his or her Social Security benefits. We will discuss this reason at length in Chapter 7.

The Social Security Actuarial Study No. 120, Period Life Tables for 2010, indicates that a healthy 62-year-old male has a 94% probability of living to age 66 and a 86% probability of living until age 70. A healthy 62-year-old female has a 96% probability of living until age 66 and a 90% chance of living until age 70. If you are age 62 and in relatively good health, the odds are overwhelmingly in your favor that you will live up to and beyond the ages of 66 and 70.

For married couples in relatively good health at age 62, the probability of at least one spouse living to age 66 is 99.8%. The probability is 98.6% that one spouse will live to age 70. Another way of looking at these statistics is to consider that there is less than a 2% chance that both the husband and wife will die before they reach the ages of 66 or 70. Because of the way the Survivor Benefit works, these statistics should be a major factor in how your claiming decision is made. If you are a married couple and both of you claim your Social Security at age 62, instead of at least one of you delaying until age 66 or age 70, because you are concerned about both of you dying before those ages, you are really going against the odds.

Let's take a look at what happens in the event that one of the spouses dies before age 66 or 70, and before he or she had a chance to claim their Social Security benefits. If we look at the married couple as a single unit, then the notion that if you delay claiming your Social Security benefits until age 66 or 70 and die before you reach those ages and end up with nothing, is incorrect. The spouse who dies may not get anything, BUT THE SURVIVING SPOUSE WILL GET SOMETHING AND WILL BE IN MUCH BETTER FINANCIAL SHAPE AS A RESULT.

CORY DIES BEFORE HE CLAIMS

Pat and Cory are married and the same age. At age 62, they consider retiring and claiming their Social Security benefits. Cory's Social Security check at his Full Retirement Age of 66 totals $1,500 per month and Pat's check is $1,000 per month. They decide that Pat will retire and claim her benefits early at age 62 and Cory will delay as long as possible and claim his Work History Benefit at age 70. Because Pat claimed her Social Security Work

History Benefit at age 62, her monthly check is reduced by 25% to $750. They decide that Cory should be the one to delay the claiming of his Social Security benefits because his check is the larger of the two.

Six years later, at age 68, Cory dies unexpectedly without claiming his Social Security benefits. Even though he died before receiving any money from Social Security, Pat will still benefit because he delayed claiming. She benefits because she can switch over to the check he would have received at the time of his death at age 68. She will receive her husband's bigger benefit for the rest of her life.

The probability is very low that an individual man or woman will die before age 66 or age 70. The probability is even lower—less than 2%—that both spouses in a married couple will die before those ages. Therefore, claiming early using this reasoning is really going against the evidence. If you are a married couple concerned about both of you dying before age 66 or 70, and both of you claim your Social Security at age 62, instead of at least one of you delaying until age 66 or 70, you are really, really going against the odds.

AFRAID YOU WILL NOT BREAK EVEN

Many retirees claim benefits early because they fear that they will not live long enough to break even. These people suggest that it is a better decision to claim early, rather than run the risk of not living long enough to make up for the money they never received while they waited to claim their benefits.

78 IS THE BREAK EVEN AGE

The term **break even age** is the age at which you will have accumulated enough Social Security income to recoup all that was foregone while you delayed claiming your benefit. A break even analysis is fairly simple math and the final result is usually the same for everyone, regardless of the amount of your Social Security benefit. If you wait until age 66 to claim your benefits, instead of claiming them at age 62, it will take you until around age 78 to break even or to make up for those four years (ages 62, 63, 64, and 65) that you did not receive any Social Security income. For married couples using the Getting Paid To Wait strategies, even if one spouse delays until age 70, the break even age is still around age 78, if not sooner. The break even age of 78 is the same for everyone who claims at age 66 instead of age 62.

Some people, after doing the break even analysis, decide to claim their benefits at age 62 because they have concluded they are not going to live to age 78. They hedge their bets and reason that delaying only makes sense if they are going to live to be older than age 78. If they die before they reach age 78, they will receive a lesser total amount of Social Security income than they would have gotten if they had claimed at 62.

ODDS ARE—YOU WILL LIVE BEYOND AGE 78

According to the latest mortality tables and life expectancy statistics, if you reach age 62 or age 66 in relatively good health, the odds that you will live beyond your break even age of 78 are much higher than the odds of you dying before that age. I know this may seem hard to believe, but it is true, and the probability is even higher that women will live beyond their break even age because, on average, women live longer than men.

CLAIMING EARLY GOES AGAINST THE ODDS

According to the Social Security Actuarial Study No. 120, Period Life Tables for 2010, a 66-year-old man has only a 33% probability of dying before age 78. That means he has a 67% chance of living beyond age 78. In other words, the odds are twice as high that a 66-year-old man will live up to and beyond age 78 as they are that he will die before age 78. A 66-year-old woman has only a 25% chance of dying before age 78, which means she has a 75% chance of living up to and beyond age 78. For a 66-year-old woman, the odds are three times as high that she will live up to and beyond age 78 as they are that she will die before age 78.

The likelihood is much higher that both the man and the woman will live beyond the breakeven age of 78. If you delay claiming your Social Security benefits until age 66 or age 70 instead of claiming them at age 62, you have a much higher chance of earning tens of thousands or even hundreds of thousands of dollars in additional Social Security income over your retirement lifetime.

THE SURVIVING SPOUSE RECEIVES THE BIGGEST BENEFIT OF DELAYING

The spouse who lives the longest will benefit the most if he or she delays claiming his or her benefits until a later age. The spouse that lives the longest benefits by receiving a bigger Survivor Benefit after the first spouse dies. We know by now that women live longer than men, and, as a result, many more women receive a Survivor Benefit than men. Making the Survivor Benefit as large as possible should be a major goal when married couples make their Social Security claiming decision. The size of the Survivor Benefit can make a huge difference in the surviving spouse's quality of life after the first spouse dies. I will show you how to make the Survivor Benefit as large as possible in Chapter 7.

CHAPTER 4 IMPORTANT CONCEPTS:

• According to the latest mortality tables and life expectancy statistics, if you reach age 62 in relatively good health, the odds are very high that you will live beyond age 66 or age 70.

• According to the latest mortality tables and life expectancy statistics, if you reach the age of 62 or 66 in relatively good health, the odds that you will live beyond your breakeven age of 78 are much higher than the odds of you dying before that age.

• With a married couple, if the spouse with the larger benefit delays claiming until age 66 or age 70 and dies before those ages, even though they never received any Social Security Benefits, they will leave their surviving spouse in much better financial shape with a larger Survivor Benefit, which the surviving spouse will receive for the rest of his or her life.

WHY WAIT FACTOR #3
SOCIAL SECURITY IS NOT GOING
AWAY ANYTIME SOON

Many people believe that our Social Security system will not be around much longer, or they doubt it will be around in its current form for the rest of their lifetime. People are being bombarded by media commentary (TV, internet, newspapers, and magazines) detailing the financial projections and funding problems that will plague the Social Security system when all the baby boomers retire and start collecting benefits. Media pundits tell us that the way our Social Security system currently works is unsustainable and that, in the near future, major changes will have to be made in order to keep it going. Most people interpret these "major changes" to mean reduced benefits. Some even think our Social Security system could become insolvent, and they will stop receiving any income at all from Social Security.

I have the utmost confidence in our Social Security system. It is the greatest anti-poverty program in the United States and has had a dramatic impact on the reduction of poverty among older people in this country. "From 1959 to 2012, the poverty rate for people age 65 and older decreased from 35% to 9%."[1] That is a huge reduction and it is primarily because of Social Security. In fact, the 9% poverty rate for people over 65 is one of the lowest poverty rates in the history of our country for people in that age bracket.[2] Some experts estimate that today, rates of poverty for people over age 65 would be as high as 45% without Social Security and the rates among women that age would be even higher.[3]

IT CAN AND WILL BE FIXED

I personally do not think the extreme outcomes discussed in the media will happen, especially for people over age 55. I certainly do not think the Social Security Administration will go out of business, nor will they stop sending out checks. There could be a reduction in benefits in the future, but that reduction would probably apply only to people younger than 55 years old at the time the change is made. However, I believe even a benefit reduction is unlikely because there are some simple fixes that the government can employ to put our Social Security system on sound financial footing for the next 75–100 years.

TOO BIG TO FAIL

For approximately one-third of all Social Security recipients (that's millions of people), their monthly Social Security check provides more than 90% of their income in retirement.[4] Without their Social Security checks, they would be left with very little or no income and would probably be destitute and homeless. For an additional one-third of recipients (more millions of people), Social Security makes up more than 50% of their retirement income.[5] For many of those people, that percentage is much higher than 50%. Therefore, approximately two-thirds, or 66%, of all Social Security recipients are either totally dependent, or critically dependent on their Social Security checks to maintain any quality of life in retirement. This is illustrated in the following chart.

PERCENTAGE OF PEOPLE DEPENDENT ON SOCIAL SECURITY

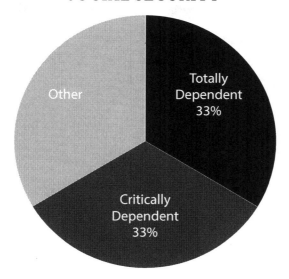

We have all heard the arguments against the viability of the Social Security system. The main contention is that Social Security was never intended to be the primary source of income for beneficiaries in retirement. The program was designed only to supplement retirees' other sources of income. This may have been the initial intention behind the program, but the reality is, too many people either depend on it completely, or depend on it for the majority of their retirement income. Because of this fact, I believe the government will make the moves necessary to fix the system. It's too big to fail.

THE WORST CASE SCENARIO

You may be skeptical that our government will eventually fix our Social Security system, so let's take a look at what happens if our government does not take the steps necessary to fix it. If the government does not take action, in the year 2033, Social Security benefits will have to be cut by about 25%. Therefore, even if our government does not do anything to fix Social Security, it does not go out of business or cease to exist. The program will continue, but only paying about 75% of the currently projected benefit. The Social Security Administration would be able to pay those reduced benefits for well over the next one hundred years. In the worst case scenario, if our government does nothing to fix Social Security, 17 years from now, benefits will have to be cut by about 25%. This will put Social Security on sound financial footing and enable it to make those reduced benefit payments well into the next century.[6]

OPTIONS TO SOLVE THE PROBLEM
WITHOUT CUTTING BENEFITS

1.) Increase FICA Taxes

Cutting benefits is one way to fix our Security System, but nobody wants to see that happen. There are a number of other simple fixes that can be implemented, which don't involve cutting anyone's benefits. When I say simple fixes, this does not mean painless fixes, especially to the millions of people who are still working. According to a 2013 Social Security Trustees Report, raising the Social Security payroll tax by approximately 2.72 percentage points split evenly between employees (1.36 percentage points) and employers (1.36 percentage points) would provide enough revenue to fully fund Social Security benefits for the next 75 years.[7]

2.) Eliminating Earnings Cap

Another simple fix is to eliminate the cap on wages. In 2016, you pay Social Security taxes (FICA on your pay stub) of 6.2% on all of your wages up to approximately $118,500. You do not pay Social Security taxes on any wages you earn over $118,500. Most people in this country make less than $118,500, so they end up paying Social Security taxes on all of their wages. Only about 6% of all the working people in this country have earnings that exceed $118,500. Many of them earn substantially more than $118,500, but they don't pay Social Security taxes on all of their wages, only the first $118,500. Simply eliminating the wages cap of $118,500 so that all workers pay Social Security taxes on all of their earnings, would go a long way toward completely fixing and fully funding the Social Security system for the next 75 years.[8]

Both of these simple fixes involve some kind of tax increase. I have never been a big fan of increasing taxes, but this is one case where I will make an exception because the quality of life for so many people is directly affected.

OTHER POTENTIAL SOLUTIONS TO THE SOCIAL SECURITY FUNDING/FINANCING PROBLEM ARE:

1. Raising the Full Retirement Age

2. Reducing the amount of the annual COLA adjustment

Because so many people are critically dependent on Social Security, I believe our government will eventually make the necessary changes to adequately fund the Social Security system. The bottom line is this: claiming your Social Security benefits at age 62 because you don't think the Social Security system is going to be around too much longer, is not a good reason to claim early.

CHAPTER 5 IMPORTANT CONCEPTS:

• Claiming your Social Security benefits at age 62 because you don't think the Social Security system is going to be around too much longer is not a good reason to claim early.

• Not fixing the Social Security system will result in about a 25% reduction in benefits in 2033, putting Social Security in the position to make those reduced benefit payments for well over 100 years.

• There are a number of simple (but not easy) fixes that would put Social Security in the position to pay benefits over the next 75 years without any benefit reductions.

• Approximately 66% of all Social Security recipients are either totally dependent or critically dependent on Social Security income.

• Some experts estimate that today, rates of poverty for people over age 65 could be as high as 45% without Social Security and the rates among women this age would be even higher.

SOURCES:

1. DeNavas-Walt, Carmen and D. Proctor, Bernadette and C. Smith, Jessica, Income, Poverty, and Health Insurance Coverage in the United States: 2012 (Washington, DC: U.S. Census Bureau, September 2013)

2. DeNavas-Walt, Carmen, Income, Poverty, and Health Insurance Coverage in the United States: 2012

3. N. Van de Water, Paul and Sherman, Arloc and Ruffing, Kathy, Social Security Keeps 22 Million Americans Out Of Poverty: A State-By-State Analysis (Washington, DC: Center on Budget and Policy Priorities, October 25, 2013)

4. Top Ten Facts About Social Security (Washington, DC: Center on Budget and Policy Priorities, November 6, 2012)

5. Top Ten Facts About Social Security

6. The 2013 Annual Report of the Board of Trustees of the Federal Old-Age and Survivors Insurance and Federal Disability Insurance Trust Funds (Washington, DC: The Board of Trustees of the Federal Old-Age and Survivors Insurance and Federal Disability Insurance Trust Funds, May 31, 2013)

7. The 2013 Annual Report of the Board of Trustees of the Federal Old-Age and Survivors Insurance and Federal Disability Insurance Trust Funds

8. John, David and Reno, Virginia, *Options For Reforming Social Security* (Washington, DC: AARP Public Policy Institute, June 24, 2012)

WHY WAIT FACTOR #4
THE PAY INCREASE BENEFIT

The Cost Of Living Adjustment feature, which is commonly referred to as COLA, usually provides Social Security recipients with a pay increase every year to help them keep up with inflation or the rising cost of living. For most retirees, this is their only way to receive a pay raise during retirement. Ideally, retirees should **maximize** the impact of the COLA feature, so they can receive the largest pay raise with the largest dollar increases possible.

Most retirees live on a **fixed income**, meaning that a retiree lives on the same amount of money or income every year. Prior to 1975, there was no provision for an automatic COLA to Social Security benefits and the size of a retiree's Social Security check remained the same year after year. In 1975, Social Security recipients began to receive COLA. Every year from 1975 until 2010, for a period of 35 years in a row, Social Security benefits were increased every year.

COLA IS TIED TO INFLATION

There was no increase in the size of Social Security checks in 2010, 2011 and 2016. According to our government, and the formula they use to track inflation, there was no inflation in the years 2009, 2010, and 2015. Because there was no inflation, there was no COLA increase on Social Security benefits for those years. This made many people very angry because the COLA feature usually is the only way they get a pay raise during their retirement. For the people who are totally dependent on Social Security, if there is no COLA increase and, consequently, no pay raise, it could make it more difficult to make ends meet.

The annual COLA increase happens automatically. If you were to consider this COLA feature a gift (because it's free), it would be one of the greatest gifts we receive from our federal government

HOW COLA WORKS

The concept of inflation is the gradual increase in cost for goods and services. Prices tend to go up every year. If you think back to the time when you bought your first car or house, both were probably a lot cheaper than a similar house or car today. In 1975, the average house in the United States cost $42,600 compared to the average house in 2013, which costs $324,500.[1] The average cost of an economy car 30 years ago was $5,866 compared to $20,000 for an economy car today.[2] In fact, everything was cheaper back then, even basic food items like milk, bread, and eggs.

When inflation rises, the cost of living goes up. COLA helps people receiving Social Security keep up with the rising cost of living, or inflation. Every year, the federal government tracks the rate of inflation in the US. There is a formula used, or an index, that determines what the general rate of inflation was for the previous year. The rate is stated in percentage terms. The inflation percentage for the previous year becomes the benchmark for the COLA percentage increase that Social Security recipients receive for the next year.

CASE STUDY: CASEY GETS A RAISE

In the year 2012, the federal government determined, based on the Inflation Index, that the inflation rate for that year was 1.7%. Casey received a COLA adjustment to her Social Security benefits. Casey saw her checks increase by 1.7% in 2013. Therefore, if Casey was receiving a Social Security check of $1,000 per month in 2012, then, in 2013, because of the COLA increase of 1.7%, Casey's monthly Social Security check increased to $1,017 per month.

In 2013, the federal government concluded that the inflation rate was 1.5% for that year. This resulted in a COLA percentage increase of the same amount and all Social Security checks increased by 1.5% in 2014. Casey, who saw her monthly Social Security check increase to $1,017 in 2013, received another COLA increase of 1.5%. Her check increased again to $1,032 per month in 2014.[3]

HOW INFLATION IMPACTS FIXED INCOMES

The average annual rate of inflation over the last 75 years has been approximately 3%, meaning that, every year, prices for goods and services have increased by an average of 3%.[4] While 3% may not seem like a very big number, over time, even a seemingly low inflation rate of 3% has a significant impact on the cost of goods and services.

TABLE 6.1

Years	0 Yrs	1 Yrs	10 Yrs	20 Yrs	24 Yrs
Percentage (%) Increase	0%	3%	34%	80%	100%
Dollar ($) Price	$1.00	$1.03	$1.34	$1.80	$2.00

After 20 years, 80 cent increase in price ($1.80 vs $1.00)
NO BIG DEAL!

Refer to Table 6.1 for an illustration of the effect that even a low rate of inflation has on the cost of goods and services over a long period of time. Starting with an item that costs $1.00 and an annual inflation rate of just 3%, after 10 years, that item will cost $1.34. After 20 years, the cost will rise to $1.80, and after 24 years, the cost will double to $2.00—a 100% increase. Even though the percentage increases over time are substantial, it may not seem like a big deal because the increase in the price of the item is pretty small. The reason the price increase is so small is because the original price of the item was very small as well, starting out at only $1.00.

SMALL INCREASES CAN HAVE A BIG IMPACT IN THE LONG RUN

TABLE 6.2

Years	0 Yrs	1 Yr	10 Yrs	20 Yrs	24 Yrs
Percentage (%) Increase	0%	3%	34%	80%	100%
Item "A"	$1.00	$1.03	$1.34	$1.80	$2.00
Item "B"	$5,000	$5,150	$6,700	$9,000	$10,000
Item "C"	$100,000	$103,000	$134,000	$180,000	$200,000

Price of Item "B" increases to $9,000 after 20 years. That's a $4,000 ($9,000 - $5,000 = $4,000) price increase. THAT IS A BIG DEAL

Price of Item "C" increases to $180,000 after 20 years. That's an $80,000 ($180,000 - $100,000 = $80,000) price increase. THAT IS AN EVEN BIGGER DEAL

In the previous example, with an annual inflation rate of 3%, an item with an original cost of $1.00 increases in price to $1.80 after 20 years. This may not seem like a very big deal because you should easily be able to pay that increased cost of only 80 cents. However, what happens if you apply that same annual inflation rate to a bigger number? Refer to Table 6.2 to see the effect of applying a small annual increase to a much larger number. While the annual percentage increase of 3% was the same as that applied to the item that only cost $1.00, item A in Table 6.2, when applied to an item that costs $5,000, item B, or one that costs $100,000, item C, over time, the total dollar amount of the increase is vastly different. You can clearly see this with the numbers circled in the 20 years column. In that column, you can see that after 20 years, the $5,000 item has increased in price to $9,000, a $4,000 increase ($9,000 - $5,000) and the $100,000 item has increased to $180,000, an $80,000 increase ($180,000 - $100,000). The original cost of the item made a significant difference in the dollar amount of the increase, 20 years later. The percentage increase for all three items was the same, but the larger the original cost, the larger the dollar increase over time.

Even at relatively low rates of inflation, the increase in the price of products can become substantial over time. If you and/or your spouse live 20-30 years in retirement, and there is a high probability that this could happen, inflation becomes a much bigger threat, simply because of longevity—the threat magnifier. (For more on inflation and longevity, see Chapter 3.)

THE COMPOUNDING EFFECT

That same relatively low rate of inflation can have a big impact on the growth of your Social Security income over time. This compounding effect is how to get the maximum value out of the COLA feature of your Social Security benefits. The larger the amount of your original Social Security benefits, the larger the dollar increase in the size of your Social Security benefit over time, because of the COLA feature.

THE BIGGER THE STARTING NUMBER, THE BIGGER THE PAY RAISE, AND THE BIGGER THE DOLLAR INCREASE IN THE SIZE OF YOUR SOCIAL SECURITY CHECK EVERY YEAR.

The following tables illustrate how you can get the most out of the COLA feature, receive larger pay raises every year, and maximize the dollar growth of your Social Security check over time. Table 6.3 shows the different Social Security benefit amounts if they are claimed at different ages. Claiming at Full Retirement Age (age 66), the benefit is $1,500. Starting benefits at age 62 reduces the amount by 25%, resulting in a monthly check of only $1,125. If you wait until age 70 to claim, the benefit increases by 32%, resulting in a monthly check of $1,980.

TABLE 6.3

Age Claimed	Amount
62	$1,125
66	$1,500
70	$1,980

CASE STUDY: CASEY BENEFITS FROM COMPOUNDING

TABLE 6.4

A	B	C
	Monthly Difference	20 Yrs Later (Assumed Annual COLA of 3%)
Age	Monthly Income	Monthly Income
62	$1,125	$2,031
66	$1,500	$2,709
Difference	$375	$678

Table 6.4 compares claiming benefits at 62 or age 66. It shows the difference in the amount of the monthly Social Security checks after 20 years. The table assumes that the COLA increases over that period of time were 3% annually. When applying the same percentage rate increase, the amount by which your Social Security check increases every year is determined by the size of the benefit that you start with. If you apply a 3% increase to a larger number, it will result in a larger increase in the dollar amount of your check.

Whether claimed at age 62 or age 66, Casey's monthly Social Security check increased by 80% over the 20-year period of time. Because the check claimed at age 66 was larger than the check claimed at age 62, it received larger dollar increases over time. In Column C of Table 6.4, after 20 years of 3% COLA increases, the difference in size between the two checks has increased to $678 per month. When they started out, in Column B, the difference between the sizes of the two checks was $375. The size of these Social Security checks grew over time only because of the COLA feature; without it, the size of the checks would have remained the same over the 20-year period. The COLA percentage applied to each check was exactly the same, but because the check claimed at age 66 ($1,500) was a larger number than the size of the check claimed at age 62 ($1,125), the check claimed at age 66 experienced higher dollar increases over that period.

TABLE 6.5

A	B	C
	Annual Difference	20 Yrs Later (Assumed Annual COLA of 3%)
Age	Annual Income	Annual Income
62	$13,500	$24,372
66	$18,000	$32,508
Difference	$4,500	$8,136

Table 6.5 shows the difference in annual income or the amount of Social Security income earned for the entire year. In Column B, you can see that the annual difference starts out at $4,500 ($18,000 - $13,500) but after 20 years of COLA adjustments, the annual difference in Column C has grown to $8,136 ($32,508 - $ 24,372).

TABLE 6.6

A	B	C
	Monthly Difference	20 Yrs Later (Assumed Annual COLA of 3%)
Age	Monthly Income	Monthly Income
62	$1,125	$2,031
70	$1,980	$3,576
Difference	$855	$1,545

Table 6.6 shows the difference in monthly income between claiming Social Security benefits at age 62 and waiting to claim them at age 70. The initial monthly difference in the size of the checks starts out at $855 ($1,980 - $1,125), as illustrated in Column B. After 20 years, in Column C, the monthly check originally claimed at age 62 has grown to $2,031, and the monthly check originally claimed at age 70 has grown to $3,576. That increases the monthly dollar difference to $1,545 ($3,570 - $2,031).

TABLE 6.7

A	B	C	
	Annual Difference	20 Yrs Later (Assumed Annual COLA of 3%)	
Age	Annual Income	Annual Income	
62	$13,500	$24,372	
70	$23,760	$42,912	
Difference	$10,260	$18,540	

Looking at the difference in annual income in Table 6.7, you see that it started out at $10,260 ($23,760 - $13,500), illustrated in Column B, but grew to a difference of $18,540 ($42,912 - $24,372), as shown in Column C, after 20 years. If Casey had claimed her benefits at age 70, her Social Security income for the year would have grown to $42,912, which is $18,540 more than the amount she would have received ($24,372) if she had claimed at age 62. The difference will be larger, the longer Casey lives.

In these illustrations, the COLA percentage was assumed to be 3%, regardless of when the Social Security benefits were claimed—between ages 62 and 70. The size of the number that the COLA percentage is applied to is what makes the big difference. By delaying the claiming of your Social Security benefits ideally until age 70, you will be able to start with the largest possible number, which will result in larger dollar increases in the amount of your Social Security check every year.

ANOTHER REASON TO DELAY

In order to take advantage of the annual COLA increases as soon as possible, you may think it would make more sense to claim your Social Security benefits as early as possible at age 62. It would appear that if you claim your benefits at age 62, you would receive eight years of annual COLA adjustments before age 70. In other words, if you wait until age 70 to claim your benefits, you will miss out on the eight years of annual COLA increases you would receive if you claimed at age 62. If that were the case, it would make the argument stronger for claiming your benefits early. However, that is not the case and because of the incredible way the COLA feature works, the argument to delay claiming your benefits as long as possible becomes even stronger.

THE SOCIAL SECURITY TIME MACHINE

Most people believe that time machines are not real and that they only exist in fantasy books, TV shows, and movies. For most of my life, I thought this was true. However, a few years ago, to my utter amazement, I discovered that a time machine does exist, within our Social Security system!

RETROACTIVE COLA CREDITS

Retroactive COLA Credits is another name for the Social Security Time Machine: they let you step back in time and take advantage of COLA increases from past years.

Delaying your benefits until age 70 will allow you to take full advantage of Retroactive COLA Credits. If you delay claiming your Social Security benefits until age 70, because of Retroactive COLA Credits, the Social Security Administration allows you to go back in time to the year when you turned age 62 and apply the COLA, from that year, to the Social Security benefit you will start to receive at age 70. This means they will increase your Social Security check by the same COLA percentage that you would have received if you had claimed your benefits when you were age 62. They will give you retroactive COLA increases for the years during which you turned age 63, 64, 65, 66, 67, 68, and 69. Social Security will go back in time and give you the COLA percentage increases for all of those past years, even though you did not claim or start your Social Security benefits until you were age 70.

You don't have to delay your benefits until age 70 to benefit from Retroactive COLA Credits. Any amount of time that you delay claiming your benefits after age 62 will allow you take advantage of the Social Security Time Machine of Retroactive COLA Credits.

CASE STUDY: CASEY DELAYS BUT STILL RECEIVES COLA INCREASES FROM PRIOR YEARS

TABLE 6.8

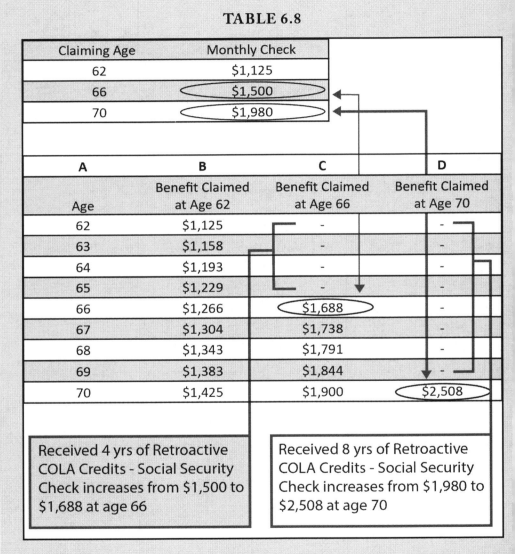

Claiming Age	Monthly Check
62	$1,125
66	$1,500
70	$1,980

A	B	C	D
Age	Benefit Claimed at Age 62	Benefit Claimed at Age 66	Benefit Claimed at Age 70
62	$1,125	-	-
63	$1,158	-	-
64	$1,193	-	-
65	$1,229	-	-
66	$1,266	$1,688	-
67	$1,304	$1,738	-
68	$1,343	$1,791	-
69	$1,383	$1,844	-
70	$1,425	$1,900	$2,508

Received 4 yrs of Retroactive COLA Credits - Social Security Check increases from $1,500 to $1,688 at age 66

Received 8 yrs of Retroactive COLA Credits - Social Security Check increases from $1,980 to $2,508 at age 70

Table 6.8 shows the amount of the Social Security benefits claimed at different ages. The Social Security benefit at the Full Retirement Age, age 66, is $1,500 per month. Claiming at age 62 reduces the benefit to $1,125 per month, and claiming at age 70 increases the benefit to $1,980 per month.

The charts assume a 3% COLA adjustment every year.

Table 6.8 shows the growth in the size of the Social Security check every year with a 3% COLA increase if benefits are claimed at age 62. It also shows how the Retroactive COLA Credits increase the size of the Social Security check when benefits are claimed at age 66 or age 70.

Under Column B, in Table 6.8, benefits were claimed at age 62. The benefits began at $1,125 per month, but every year, the size of the monthly check increased by 3%, and at age 66, the size of the monthly check grew to $1,266 per month. At age 70, their monthly check grew to $1,425 per month.

Column C, in Table 6.8, shows what happens when Social Security benefits are claimed at age 66. Instead of receiving $1,500 per month at age 66, because of Retroactive COLA Credits, Casey's monthly check is increased to $1,688. The Social Security Administration went back in time to the year in which Casey was 62 years old and credited her with the COLA increase for that year. They did the same thing for the years in which she was age 63, 64, and 65 years old. They gave Casey four years of Retroactive COLA increases, which increased the size of her monthly check to $1,688, when she claimed her benefits at age 66.

Column D, in Table 6.8, shows what happens if Social Security benefits are delayed and claimed at age 70. Claiming Social Security benefits at age 70 results in receiving eight years of Retroactive COLA Credits, which increases the size of the monthly check from $1,980 to $2,508. By delaying the claiming of Social Security until age 70, and because of Retroactive COLA Credits, the size of the Social Security check, starting at age 70, has grown to $2,508.

TABLE 6.9

A	B	C
Claiming Age	Monthly Check	Monthly Check at Age 70 with Retroactive COLA Credits
62	$1,125	$1,425
70	$1,980	$2,508
Difference	$855	$1,083

Table 6.9 compares the difference between the size of the original checks claimed at age 62 of $1,125, and at age 70 of $1,980. That difference starts out at $855 ($1,980 - $1,125) in Column B. Eight years later, the check originally claimed at age 62, has grown to $1,425. The check claimed at age 70, because of eight years of Retroactive COLA Credits, has grown to $2,508. Because the difference in the size of the two checks has grown from $855 to $1,083, this will further reduce the break even age between claiming early or delaying.

There is no disadvantage to waiting and claiming benefits at a later age. In fact, because of Retroactive COLA Credits, it makes the case even stronger to delay claiming.

INFLATION PROTECTION CAN BE BOUGHT

Some investment products are specifically designed to provide income for investors, especially retirees. Some of those products give the investor the option of purchasing an inflation rider, which is similar to Social Security's COLA. If an inflation rider is purchased, the income distributions will increase every year, usually by a stated percentage. I use the word purchase because the investor incurs an additional cost to obtain an inflation rider. Many investors decide against purchasing the inflation rider because they think the cost of it is too expensive. By contrast, the COLA feature of Social Security is free of charge, which makes it one of the greatest gifts from our government.

YOU HAVE THE WISDOM OF THE AGES

I told you earlier that there was no COLA increase in the years 2010, 2011 and 2016. That really upset a lot of people. Fear not, inflation came back and all Social Security recipients received a COLA increase of 3.6%, in 2012. I can almost guarantee you that most of the angry people did not understand how important the COLA feature was when they made their Social Security claiming decision. More than likely, the vast majority didn't even consider it. Had these retirees maximized the benefit of COLA—which would have resulted in much bigger pay raises and larger dollar increases every year in the size of their Social Security check—their financial life could have been much easier. Unfortunately, many of these people claimed their Social Security benefits at age 62, and they received the smallest pay raises and the smallest dollar increases possible, every year.

When most of these people claimed their Social Security benefits, they did not have the wisdom of the ages. It was only many years after receiving their Social Security checks when they realized the importance of the COLA feature. If they had this wisdom before they claimed, they may have made a different decision. They may have decided to delay claiming their benefits as long as possible, in order to take full advantage of the COLA feature.

THERE IS NO DISADVANTAGE TO WAITING AND CLAIMING BENEFITS AT A LATER AGE. IN FACT, BECAUSE OF RETROACTIVE COLA CREDITS, IT MAKES THE CASE EVEN STRONGER TO DELAY CLAIMING.

You have the wisdom of the ages, and you have it at the right time; before you make your Social Security claiming decision. More and more people are choosing to delay claiming their Social Security benefits. It is my hope that you will be one of those people who lock in the biggest pay raises and receive the biggest dollar increases possible. This is why you need to give the COLA feature the important consideration it deserves before you make your claiming decision. It could make a very big difference in maintaining a good quality of life and financial independence throughout your retirement.

CHAPTER 6 IMPORTANT CONCEPTS:

• When inflation rises, the cost of living goes up. COLA helps all people receiving Social Security benefits keep up with inflation or the rising cost of living.

• The COLA feature provides all Social Security recipients with the opportunity to receive an increase in the dollar amount of their monthly benefit check, every year.

• All Social Security recipients receive the same COLA percentage increase, but if that same percentage is applied to a larger benefit number, it will result in larger dollar increases every year for the rest of your life.

• If you delay claiming your Social Security benefits as long as possible, ideally until age 70, the annual COLA increases will be applied to a larger benefit number and provide you with larger dollar increases for the rest of your life, and, if married, possibly for the rest of your spouse's life as well.

• Retroactive COLA Credits allow you to recapture the pay increases you deferred while you delayed claiming you Social Security benefits.

• There is no disadvantage to waiting and claiming benefits at a later age. Because of Retroactive COLA Credits, the case is even stronger to delay claiming.

SOURCES:

1. Median and Average Sales Prices of New Homes Sold in United States (Washington, DC: United States Census Bureau)

2. History and Prices for Models for Autos in the 70s (United States: The People History, 2004)

3. History of Automatic Coat of Living Adjustments (United States: SSA, 2014)

4. Historical Inflation Rates: 1914-2014

WHY WAIT FACTOR #5
THE SURVIVOR BENEFIT

IS A CAREFREE RETIREMENT POSSIBLE?

Social Security's Survivor Benefit is potentially the greatest gift one spouse can give the other. There is a very good chance that one spouse in a married couple could end up completely dependent on the Survivor Benefit from Social Security in order to maintain his or her quality of life after the other spouse passes away. That's why every married couple should try to make the Survivor Benefit as big as possible.

For many Americans, retirement would be difficult without income from Social Security. Because the earliest a person can claim Social Security is age 62, people often choose to retire at 62. A married couple will often do a simple financial analysis of their expenses and income sources before choosing to retire. They add up their monthly bills or expenses, and then add up their sources of income, including their two checks from Social Security. If their monthly income (including Social Security) will be enough to pay all their monthly bills, many couples make a decision to retire and claim Social Security at age 62. In fact, they may have more than enough income to pay all their monthly bills, leaving money left over to do some fun things in retirement. At this point, they may think life is good and the future seems bright. I encourage you to examine your situation more thoroughly!

THE TOUGH QUESTIONS:

• What happens when one of us dies?

• Will the surviving spouse still be able to pay all of the monthly bills when he or she receives only one check from Social Security: the Survivor Benefit check?

• Will there be any money left over to enjoy life or pay for unexpected expenses that may arise?

THE ONE QUESTION THAT NO COUPLE WANTS TO ASK:

WHAT HAPPENS WHEN ONE OF US DIES?

It's not a question of *if*, it is a question of when. When one spouse passes away, what happens to the surviving spouse's Social Security income and how will it impact his or her ability to pay the bills and maintain a good quality of life? This is an unpleasant question, but one that all married couples need to address. Oftentimes, this issue is not considered when the claiming decision is being made, which results in a much smaller Survivor Benefit. Many times it even results in the Surviving Spouse trying to make ends meet with the smallest Survivor Benefit possible.

The Survivor Benefit is usually more important, many times critically important, for women because, according to the National Vital Statistic Report from the Division of Vital Statistics, men typically die before women. That being the case, many more women receive the Survivor Benefit than men.

HOW THE SURVIVOR BENEFIT WORKS— THE SMALLER CHECK GOES AWAY

Let's take a look at how the Survivor Benefit works. The Social Security Administration states that in 2012, the average annual Social Security income received by women 65 years and older was $12,520, versus $16,398 for men. A married couple receives two Social Security checks, one made payable to the husband and one made payable to the wife. The husband's check is usually bigger and he also usually dies first. After the husband dies, the surviving wife will stop receiving her smaller check and continue to receive her deceased husband's bigger check. Her husband's bigger check is the Survivor Benefit. If the wife dies before her husband, the husband will continue to receive his bigger check, and his wife's smaller check will stop coming after her death.

Even though it is the smaller of the two checks that is no longer received, the surviving spouse, in this case, the wife, is left with a substantial reduction of her Social Security income of 33%–50%. A 33%–50% reduction in Social Security income after the first spouse's passing could make life very difficult for the surviving spouse.

Married couples should give the **Survivor Benefit** major consideration before they make their Social Security claiming decision. The claiming decision of the spouse with the bigger benefit will have a direct impact on the size of the Survivor Benefit. Making the Survivor Benefit as large as possible will play a critical role in the surviving spouse maintaining a good quality of life after the first spouse dies.

CASE STUDY: CRIS AND LEE GET STRATEGIC WITH THE SURVIVOR BENEFIT

When Cris and Lee both claim their Social Security benefits, they will receive two Social Security checks—one made payable to Lee and the other made payable to Cris. Cris has the bigger Full Retirement Age Benefit of $1,500 per month, compared to Lee's Full Retirement Age Benefit of only $1,000. Assuming Cris dies first, Lee will then receive only Cris's larger check. Even though her Social Security check was smaller than Cris's, she is not required to continue to receive the smaller check. **Lee can switch over to Cris's larger Social Security check, which is considered the Survivor Benefit.** If Lee died first, Cris would continue to receive his larger monthly check, and Lee's smaller check would stop coming.

TABLE 7.1

A	B	C	D	E	F
Cris's Claiming Age	Cris's Check at Age 82	**Lee's Check at Age 82	Cris and Lee's Total Combined Income [Two Checks B+C]	Monthly Survivor Benefit (Cris Dies at 82 yrs) [One Check]	Yearly Survivor Benefit (Cris Dies at 82 yrs)
62	$2,031	$1,354	$3,385	$2,235***	$26,820
66	$2,709	$1,354	$4,063	$2,709	$32,508
70	$3,576	$1,354	$4,930	$3,576	$42,912

Much easier for Lee to live on this income after Cris dies.

*Assumed an annual COLA increase of 3.00%.

**Column "C" - Lee's smaller check will stop after Cris dies at age 82.

***Minimum Survivor Benefit when Cris claimed at age 62.

In Table 7.1, Column A lists Cris's three different claiming ages of 62, 66, or 70. I have assumed that Cris and Lee are the same age. Column B shows the size of Cris's monthly check when he reaches age 82. The size of his checks grew to these higher monthly amounts because of a COLA adjustment of 3% every year. Column C shows the size of Lee's check at age 82. In each scenario, I have assumed Lee claimed her benefit at age 62, and that's why all the amounts are the same $1,354, in Column C.

In Column D, Cris and Lee's Total Combined Monthly Income column, both monthly checks are added together to arrive at the combined monthly total. Column D illustrates that when Cris claimed his benefits at age 62, their combined income 20 years later, at age 82, assuming they both are still alive, is $3,385 per month. At this point, you may be thinking that they should be able to live fairly comfortably on that amount of money. You are probably right considering $3,385 every month or $40,620 per year is an amount of money that will support most people's retirement lifestyle. As long as both Cris and Lee are alive, they will continue to receive this amount of Social Security income. In fact, because of annual COLA increases, their Social Security income should increase every year.

THE MONTHLY SURVIVOR BENEFIT WHEN CRIS DIES— HE CLAIMED AT 62

What happens when one of the spouses dies? Column E, the Monthly Survivor Benefit (Cris Dies at age 82) column, shows what happens if Cris dies at age 82. Lee will receive only one check from Social Security. She can switch to her Survivor Benefit and receive the amount of her husband's larger check. If Cris claimed his Social Security benefits at age 62, then 20 years later, after he died at age 82, Lee will receive only one monthly Survivor Benefit check of $2,235, and her smaller check of $1,354 stops. She is facing a substantial reduction in her Social Security income. When her smaller check of $1,354 stops coming, it reduces the monthly income from $3,385 (Column D) to $2,235 per month (Column E). Column F, Yearly Survivor Benefit (Cris Dies at age 82), shows the amount of Social Security income Lee will receive for the year is reduced to $26,820.

IF CRIS CLAIMED AT 66

If Cris had delayed claiming his Social Security benefits until age 66 or age 70, Lee's Survivor Benefit would be substantially larger. If you look at the middle row of numbers for age 66, you see, in Column E, the effect of Cris delaying his claim until age 66. After he died at age 82, Lee's monthly Survivor Benefit would be $2,709 per month, as compared to $2,235 if he claimed his benefits at age 62. The higher monthly Social Security check provided Lee with more yearly Social Security income as shown in Column F—$32,508 compared to $26,820.

IF CRIS CLAIMED AT 70

The difference is even greater if Cris had waited until he was 70 years old to claim his Social Security benefits. The bottom row of numbers in Table 7.1 show what happens to the Survivor Benefit if Cris had waited until age 70 to claim his benefits. If he had claimed at age 70, when he died at age 82, the Survivor Benefit in Column E would be $3,576 per month or $42,912 per year (Column F), compared to $2,235 per month or $26,820 per year if he had claimed at age 62. Lee would receive a substantially larger Survivor Benefit from Social Security if Cris claimed his benefits at age 70, instead of age 62.

HOW THE SURVIVOR BENEFIT IMPACTS
THE CLAIMING DECISION

Most married couples are either unaware of the Survivor Benefit and how it works, or they simply do not realize its importance. As a result, many married couples make a Social Security claiming decision that minimizes the size of the Survivor Benefit. After the first spouse passes away and the surviving spouse is left with the Survivor Benefit, only then does the critical importance of the Survivor Benefit become obvious. However, by that time, it is too late to do anything about it. The time to carefully consider the Survivor Benefit, and make it as large as possible, is the time when the couple is making their Social Security claiming decision. Better claiming decisions can create a sufficient Survivor Benefit, enabling financial independence and a better quality of life to the survivor.

TWO CHECKS IN ONE

By delaying claiming until age 70, the higher-earning spouse can often leave a surviving spouse ONE Survivor Benefit check that is larger than the combined total of the TWO checks the couple would have received had they both claimed their benefits at age 62. When claimed strategically, the Survivor Benefit can be like receiving **TWO** checks in **ONE**.

TABLE 7.2

A	B	C	D	E	F
Cris's Claiming Age	Cris's Monthly Check at Age 82	** Lee's Monthly Check at Age 82	Cris and Lee's Total Combined Income [Two Checks B+C]	Monthly Survivor Benefit (Cris Dies at 82 yrs) [One Check]	Yearly Survivor Benefit (Cris Dies at 82 yrs)
62	$2,031	$1,354	$3,385	$2,235***	$26,820
70	$3,576	$1,354	$4,930	$3,576	$42,912

It's like TWO checks in ONE. ONE check of $3,576 (Survivor Benefit) in Column "E" is bigger than the combined total of $3,385 from TWO checks in Column "D".

*Assumed an annual COLA increase of 3.00%.

**Column "C" - Lee's smaller check will stop after Cris dies at age 62.

***Minimum Survivor Benefit Cris claimed at age 62.

In Table 7.2, there are only two claiming ages, age 62 and age 70. All the numbers for the two claiming ages of 62 or 70 in Table 7.2 are exactly the same as the numbers in Table 7.1. The number circled in Column D, represents the combined total of the TWO checks Cris and Lee received when they were both alive and just before Cris died. The number circled in Column E, $3,576, represents the amount of the ONE Survivor Benefit check the wife receives after her husband dies at age 82.

When Cris claimed his Social Security benefits at age 70, the size of the ONE Survivor Benefit check of $3,576 in Column E is larger than the combined $3,385 total of the TWO checks in Column D that Cris and Lee received when they both claimed their benefits at age 62. This is how the higher-earning spouse can leave the lower-earning spouse a Survivor Benefit that's like getting TWO checks in ONE.

The higher-earning spouse claiming at age 70 doesn't guarantee that the one Survivor Benefit check will be as big as the combined total of the two checks they would receive if they claimed at age 62. However, in the majority of cases, that is the result.

WHAT HAPPENS IF ONE SPOUSE DIES BEFORE BENEFITS BEGIN?

"What if I delay claiming and die before I start to collect my Social Security benefits?" I first addressed this question in Chapter 4, when I shared with you the very high probability of a man or women living to age 66 and age 70. With a married couple, there is a second part to the answer for that question, and it involves the Survivor Benefit. Let's take a look at what happens in the event that one spouse dies before age 66 or 70, and before he or she had a chance to claim their Social Security benefits. If we look at the married couple as a single unit, then the notion that you end up with nothing if you delay claiming your Social Security benefits until age 66 or 70, and die before you reach those ages is incorrect. The spouse who dies may not get anything, but the surviving spouse will get something and will be in much better financial shape as a result.

CASE STUDY: CORY DIES BEFORE HE CLAIMS

In Chapter 4, we first encountered Pat and Cory, who are married and the same age. You may recall Pat retired and claimed her benefits early at age 62. Her check is $750 per month. They decided that Cory would delay claiming his benefits until age 70 because his check was the larger of the two. Cory's Social Security check at his Full Retirement Age of 66 totaled $1,500 per month. Cory died unexpectedly at age 68, without claiming his benefits and before receiving any money from Social Security. Pat still benefited from his delayed claim. She switched over to the check Cory would have received at his date of death. She will receive her husband's bigger benefit for the rest of her life.

PAT AND CORY BOTH CLAIM AT 62

Let's compare this scenario—where the husband dies before he had a chance to claim his benefit—to one in which both the husband and wife claim their benefits at age 62.

TABLE 7.3

Pat's Full Retirement Age Benefit - $1,000. Cory's Full Retirement Age Benefit - $1,500.								
Age	62	63	64	65	66	67	68	69	70
Cory's Monthly Benefit	$1,125	$1,125	$1,125	$1,125	$1,125	$1,125	*	-	-
Pat's Monthly Benefit	$750	$750	$750	$750	$750	$750	$1,237	$1,237	$1,237

* Cory dies at age 68

After Cory dies, Pat claims a Survivor Benefit of $1,237 per month.

Table 7.3 illustrates Pat and Cory claiming their benefits at age 62. Their Full Retirement Age Benefits are $1,000 per month for Pat and $1,500 for Cory, but because they both claimed their benefits at age 62, the amount is reduced to $750 per month for Pat and $1,125 for Cory. They receive these same benefits up until the day Cory dies at age 68. After he dies, Pat can claim a Survivor Benefit based on her husband's larger benefit and receive

$1,237 per month. If she does this, her smaller benefit of $750 per month stops, as you see in the Age 68 column.

In this situation, Pat's Survivor Benefit is increased from $1,125 per month to $1,237 per month because Social Security pays the surviving spouse a minimum Survivor Benefit of 82.5% of the deceased spouse's Full Retirement benefit. When Cory claimed his benefits at age 62, he received 75% of his Full Retirement Age Benefit or $1,125. After he died, because Social Security pays the surviving spouse a minimum Survivor Benefit of 82.5% of the deceased spouse's Full Retirement benefit, they increased the amount of the Survivor Benefit up to $1,237 per month. She will receive that Survivor Benefit of $1,237 per month starting at age 68 for the rest of her life.

CORY DIES AT 68 WITHOUT CLAIMING, PAT CLAIMS AT 62

TABLE 7.4

Age	62	63	64	65	66	67	68	69	70
Pat's Full Retirement Age Benefit - $1,000. Cory's Full Retirement Age Benefit - $1,500.									
Cory's Monthly Benefit	$0	$0	$0	$0	$0	$0	*	-	-
Pat's Monthly Benefit	$750	$750	$750	$750	$750	$750	$1,740	$1,740	$1,740

* Cory dies at age 68

After Cory dies at age 68, Pat switches to the benefit Cory would have received at age 68 of $1,740 in the form of a Survivor Benefit.

Table 7.4 shows you what happens if Cory delayed claiming and died before his benefits began. In this case, as in Table 7.3, Pat claims her reduced benefit of $750 per month at age 62. Cory plans to wait until he is age 70 to claim his benefit and that's why there are zeros in all the age columns for his monthly benefit. At age 68, Cory dies before he has a chance to claim his Social Security benefit. Even though he never received any Social Security income while he was alive, Pat will benefit greatly as a result of his delaying the claiming of his benefits. Under the Age 68 column, you see that after Cory's death at age 68, Pat switches from her own smaller benefit of $750 per month to her Survivor Benefit of $1,740 per month. The widow's Survivor Benefit is $1,740 per month because that is the amount of the monthly Social Security check Cory would have received at the time of his death at age 68. The husband's check was $1,740 per month because, for every year he delayed after his Full Retirement Age of 66, he received Delayed Retirement Credits and his benefit grew by 8% per year. In this case, he was 68 when he died, which was two years past his Full Retirement Age of 66, so his benefit would increase by 16% (2 x 8% = 16%). Increasing his Full Retirement Age Benefit of $1,500 by 16% brings it up to $1,740 per month.

Even though Cory never received any of his Social Security benefits, Pat is left in much better financial condition because her monthly Social Security Survivor benefit check is $1,740. If Cory had claimed his benefits at age 62, like he did in Table 7.3, when he died, Pat's monthly Survivor Benefit check would have only totaled $1,237. We know that there is a high probability that the surviving wife could live for another 20 to 25 years and the much higher Survivor Benefit check of $1,740 per month will also receive bigger dollar increases every year because of the COLA feature. It is unfortunate that Cory died before he claimed his Social Security benefits, but the bigger Survivor Benefit he left his wife should make her life much easier and is one of the greatest gifts he could ever give her.

SOMETIMES THE OBVIOUS CHOICE ISN'T THE BEST CHOICE

Let's again assume Pat and Cory are the same age and, at age 62, they are both considering retiring. Pat's Social Security benefit at her Full Retirement Age of 66 is $1,600 per month, and Cory's benefit at his Full Retirement Age is $1,400 per month. Pat really likes her job and instead of retiring at age 62 and receiving a reduced monthly check, she decides to continue to work until age 66 and claim her Social Security benefits at that time. Because Pat has decided to work until age 66, Cory decides to continue to work also and claim his benefits at age 66.

In this case, Cory dies just before his 66th birthday and prior to either spouse claiming their Social Security benefits. Pat still wants to retire at age 66 and claim her benefits then. She has a choice of which Social Security benefit to claim: either her own Work History Benefit of $1,600 per month, or Cory's Survivor Benefit check of $1,400 per month.

You may think the decision is obvious: she should take the $1,600 monthly check based on her work history. Believe it or not, that's probably not the best choice. This is where the flexibility of the Survivor Benefit comes into play. If Pat takes Cory's check in the form of a Survivor Benefit of $1,400 per month, she can continue to delay the claiming of her own Social Security Work History Benefit. By doing so, the size of her own unclaimed Work History Benefit check will continue to earn Delayed Retirement Credits and grow by 8% per year for every year that she delays after her Full Retirement Age of 66. She can continue to delay up until age 70, which would maximize the size of her own monthly Work History Benefit check, increasing it from $1,600 per month up to $2,112 per month. If she claims the monthly Survivor Benefit check of $1,400 per month, she has the option of switching over to her own Work History Benefit at any time up until the age of 70.

TABLE 7.5

Age	62	63	64	65	66	67	68	69	70
Cory's Monthly Benefit	$0	$0	$0	$0	*	-	-	-	-
Pat's Monthly Benefit	$0	$0	$0	$0	$1,600	$1,600	$1,600	$1,600	$1,600

Pat's Full Retirement Age benefit - $1,600. Cory's Full Retirement Age benefit - $1,400.

* Cory dies at age 66

Pat claims her own Work History Benefit of $1,600 per month.

Table 7.5 shows you what the numbers look like if Pat claims her own Work History Benefit at age 66. Pat does what appears to be the obvious choice and claims her own Work History Benefit of $1,600 per month, at age 66, and she receives that benefit for the rest of her life.

TABLE 7.6

Age	62	63	64	65	66	67	68	69	70
Cory's Monthly Benefit	$0	$0	$0	$0	*	-	-	-	-
Pat's Monthly Benefit	$0	$0	$0	$0	$1,400	$1,400	$1,400	$1,400	$2,112

Pat's Full Retirement Age Benefit - $1,600. Cory's Full Retirement Age Benefit - $1,400.

* Cory dies at age 66

Pat claims Cory's benefit of 1,400 as a Survivor Benefit.

Pat switches to her own 'Maxed Out' Work History Benefit of $2,112 for the rest of her life.

In Table 7.6, after Cory dies at age 66, Pat claims a Survivor Benefit of $1,400 per month. This $1,400 per month is the amount Cory would have received at his Full Retirement Age of 66. By claiming the Survivor Benefit at age 66, she delays claiming her own Work History Benefit, and as a result, earns Delayed Retirement Credits, allowing her benefit to grow by 8% per year. She collects the $1,400 per month ($16,800 per year) for a period of four years when she is age 66, 67, 68, and 69. At age 70, she switches from her Survivor Benefit of $1,400 per month to her maxed-out Work History Benefit of $2,112 per month, which she receives for the rest of her life.

Because she could take advantage of Cory's Survivor Benefit, Pat was able to delay her own Work History Benefit until age 70. By delaying her Work History Benefit until age 70, she maximized her benefit and locked in the largest check she could receive from Social Security for the rest of her life.

A surviving wife has a pretty good chance of living 20 to 25 years in her retirement. I think you would agree that receiving a check from Social Security every month totaling $2,112 would make life a lot easier than receiving a check totaling only $1,600. In fact, if they had both claimed benefits at age 62, like many married couples do, her monthly Social Security check would have been only $1,200. In this case, the combination of delaying, along with the flexibility of the Survivor Benefit should make Pat's life a lot easier after the death of her husband, at least from a financial perspective.

WHAT IF YOU ARE ALREADY A WIDOW OR WIDOWER?

If you are already a widow or widower and haven't claimed your Social Security benefits, you could have a number of different claiming options available to you. You need to know what those options are because correctly timing when you claim a Survivor Benefit or your own Work History Benefit could greatly increase your Social Security income.

In order to make sure you are aware of the best options or claiming strategy for your personal situation, you should go to my website at www.Getting-PaidToWait.com and use my Social Security Calculator. After you input a couple of pieces of information, it will show you a suggested claiming strategy that should maximize your Social Security income. The whole process should take less than a minute, and could make a huge difference in the amount of Social Security income you receive over your retirement lifetime.

HOW SOON CAN YOU CLAIM THE SURVIVOR BENEFIT?

You can claim a Survivor Benefit as early as age 60 (age 50 if you are disabled and even younger than that if you have minor children), but if you claim that early, your benefit will be reduced. In fact, if you claim any time before your Full Retirement Age (assumed age 66), your Survivor Benefit will be reduced. The amount of the reduction in your benefit decreases the closer you get to your Full Retirement Age. There is a chart on the Social Security Administration website (www.ssa.gov) that will show you the percentage reductions in your Survivor Benefit at claiming ages younger than Full Retirement Age.

GETTING PAID TO WAIT—HOW TO MAXIMIZE THE SURVIVOR BENEFIT

The spouse who will receive the larger check from Social Security should delay claiming their Social Security benefit as long as possible, ideally until age 70. If delaying until age 70 is not feasible, then the spouse should delay for as many years after age 62 as possible. If the higher earning spouse makes a poor decision and claims his benefits at age 62, it's usually the woman who suffers the consequences because there is a very high probability that she will outlive her husband, and she will have to survive on the much smaller Survivor Benefit check. The husband usually receives the bigger Social Security benefit and that is why his claiming decision is usually the most important financial decision in his wife's lifetime. Leaving his wife with a much bigger Survivor Benefit could be the greatest gift a husband could give to his wife, a gift that his surviving wife will cherish for the rest of her life.

CHAPTER 7 IMPORTANT CONCEPTS:

• Married couples should give the Survivor Benefit major consideration before they make their Social Security claiming decision because one spouse may be totally dependent on the Survivor Benefit after the first spouse dies. The timing of the claiming decision has a direct impact on the size of the Survivor Benefit.

• The Survivor Benefit is usually more important, many times critically important, for the woman because, according to the National Vital Statistic Report from the Division of Vital Statistics, men typically die before women.

• Regardless of when the first spouse passes away, the surviving spouse will be left with a much larger Survivor Benefit if the spouse with the larger Social Security Work History Benefit, delays claiming at least until age 66, but preferably, until age 70.

• By delaying the claiming of Social Security benefits until age 70, the higher-earning spouse creates the biggest Survivor Benefit possible.

WHY WAIT FACTOR #6
TOO MANY WOMEN STRUGGLE
FINANCIALLY

I wrote this book for two reasons: one, to give people quality advice on when and how they should claim their Social Security benefits and, secondly, to raise awareness of the issue of how many single women over the age of 65 struggle financially or live in poverty and how making a better Social Security claiming decision could greatly reduce the problem. I hope to start a national conversation about this important issue and greatly reduce the number of women who struggle financially!

SOME STATISTICS ABOUT WOMEN OVER 62:

1.) The percentage of married women over the age of 65 who live in poverty is approximately 5%.[1]

2.) The percentage of widowed women over the age of 65 who live in poverty is approximately 15%.[2]

3.) By age 62, 56% of Social Security recipients are women; by age 85, that number grows to 66%.[3]

4.) In 2012, 50% of all older unmarried females receiving Social Security benefits relied on Social Security for 90% or more of their income.[4]

5.) There are three times more women who are still alive in their 90s than there are men.[5]

6.) Poverty rates among older, single women, who were either never married or divorced, are even higher than those for older widowed women.[6]

THE STRATEGY FOR SINGLE WOMEN WHO HAVE NEVER BEEN MARRIED

The best strategy for single women, who were never married, is to delay claiming their Social Security benefits as long as possible in order to maximize their Work History Benefit.

THE STRATEGY FOR WOMEN WHO ARE DIVORCED

Women who were married for more than 10 years before they were divorced have more claiming options than women who never married. Divorced women over age 65 have some of the highest rates of poverty in this country, so it is critical that they are aware of all the claiming options that are available. Those options could pay a critical role in helping them maintain a decent quality of life in retirement. These claiming options are also available to divorced men. Claiming options for divorced spouses who were married for at least 10 years before their divorce are illustrated in Chapter 14.

MARRIED WOMEN DO OKAY, WHILE MANY WIDOWED WOMEN STRUGGLE

Married women over age 65 do much better in retirement than single women. The percentage of married women over the age of 65 who live in poverty is approximately 5%. This is one of the lowest poverty rates for any age demographic in this country. The major reason why it is so low is because while both spouses are alive, they receive two Social Security checks. Life is pretty good from a financial perspective. However, that changes after one of the spouses dies. We have already established that it is the husband who usually dies first, and by age 85, two out of three Social Security recipients are women. So, by age 85, there are twice as many women still alive than there are men. After the husband dies, the probability that his widowed wife will struggle financially, increases dramatically. The percentage of widowed women over the age of 65 living in poverty, is approximately 15%. The major reason for the increase is because after the husband dies, the surviving widow receives only one Social Security check: the Survivor Benefit. Oftentimes, the amount of the one Survivor Benefit check isn't large enough and the widowed wife ends up struggling financially. In many cases, the Survivor Benefit isn't enough because the deceased husband claimed his benefit too early and left his widowed wife with the smallest Survivor Benefit possible.

THE STRATEGY FOR MARRIED COUPLES

Social Security claiming decisions for married couples should be given careful consideration by both spouses. When to claim and the potential consequences of claiming choices must be explored and discussed in a very honest way. The higher-earning spouse, which statistically is the husband, making the wrong Social Security claiming decision could have an enormous negative impact on the retirement security of the lower-earning spouse. Delaying the claiming of the higher-earning spouse's Social Security benefit as long as possible could result in considerably more Social Security income during a married couple's lifetime and a larger Survivor Benefit for the surviving spouse. If the higher-earning spouse waits until age 66, or until age 70, to claim his Social Security benefits, the Survivor Benefit he will leave to his surviving spouse will be much larger than what he would leave if he claimed his benefits at age 62. This much larger Survivor Benefit could play a critical role in preventing the surviving spouse from struggling financially after the first spouse dies.

WOMEN ARE MORE LIKELY TO BE WIDOWED IN RETIREMENT THAN MEN, SO GOOD CLAIMING CHOICES MADE BY THE HUSBAND AND WIFE CAN REDUCE THE PROBABILITY OF A WIDOWED WOMAN STRUGGLING FINANCIALLY AFTER THE HUSBAND PASSES AWAY.

CASE STUDY: BILL AND JILL

Bill and Jill are both college graduates of the same age. When this story begins, they do not know each other. After college, both Bill and Jill get good jobs working for large companies in a major city in the United States. Each has their own apartment, a nice circle of friends, and is excited about the bright future ahead.

After a few years, Bill and Jill meet on a blind date. They fall in love and get married, and their lives improve in every way! Instead of paying rent for two apartments, they now only pay rent for one. Over the next couple of years, they each receive promotions and pay increases at work, making for a growing dual-income household. Bill and Jill take nice vacations, go out for dinner often, and buy nice things for their apartment. After a couple of years of married bliss, they decide to start a family. They have saved some money, which they use for a down payment on a house in the suburbs, in a town with a great school system.

Bill and Jill moved into their new home and were overjoyed to discover that they are expecting their first child! Together, they made the choice for Jill to stay home with their baby for six months after she is born. After six months, Jill returns to work as planned. Their expenses have increased dramatically since moving to the suburbs. Their mortgage payment is much larger than the rent payment on their apartment, their commuting expenses are double, and they now have expenses for childcare.

After Jill returned to work, Bill and Jill were satisfied at first with the child-care they had chosen. However, as time went by, they began to realize it did not compare to their child having constant, nurturing care from her mother. Jill became torn by the need to provide for her family and the yearning to be a full-time mother. Jill turns down promotions and big projects at work, because it would require her to work more hours, which would mean less time with the baby. Even though it would mean more money, it is not worth it to her.

After a couple of years, Bill and Jill decide to have another baby. During the time between the birth of their two children, Bill continues to do well at work. He is promoted and given increased responsibility, which results in his working more hours, but also making more money. Because Bill is doing so well at work, they are able to make ends meet on Bill's income alone. So, Bill and Jill decide that Jill will stop working until both children start school.

After their second child enters kindergarten, Jill reenters the workforce. She gets a job, but it amounts to starting over again. Her income is much lower than her husband's, because during the time that she stayed home with the children, he continued to advance in his career with promotions and raises. For many years, Jill sacrificed her career in order to raise their children in the manner that both Bill and Jill had always hoped for.

Jill is very talented, but has to turn down promotions and big projects at work once again because the time commitment will interfere with their children's busy schedule of after school activities. Jill has to carefully balance her work and family obligations in order to meet all the expectations of those around her. She regularly attends or transports her children to sporting events, dance recitals, art lessons, and Boy Scout troop meetings. Because of Bill's heavy work schedule, he can't attend every event the children are involved in, but he gets to as many as he can. They are both great parents and both love not only each other, but their children dearly.

Even though Jill's top priority is her family, she still works very hard at her job and is offered a big promotion with a substantial increase in income, which she turns down, because it would require them to move to a different city. Moving did not make sense because Bill was earning far more income than Jill, since he had an extremely successful and uninterrupted career.

BILL AND JILL IN THEIR EARLY 60s

Bill and Jill put their children through college and both are gainfully employed and self-supporting. Bill and Jill are in their early 60s and are considering retirement. Although Bill has done well in his career, he is looking forward to retiring at age 62, and collecting his Social Security benefits. Jill will follow Bill into retirement at age 62 (they are both the same age). They both claim their Social Security benefits at age 62, but Bill's Social Security check is much larger than Jill's check because he was the higher-earning spouse in their marriage, while Jill was the spouse who made the compromises in her career for the sake of her family. Jill looks forward to spending her retirement years with Bill. Their two Social Security checks, combined with some savings they have accumulated over the years, should make their retirement fairly comfortable.

For many years, Bill and Jill have a comfortable retirement. Sometime in Bill's late 70s or early 80s, he experiences a negative health event and becomes ill. His illness gets progressively worse. They consider putting him in a nursing home, but decide he should stay at home. Jill cares for him.

JILL IS ALONE AND STRUGGLING

Over the next couple of years, Jill takes care of Bill, who gets progressively worse. The time comes when Jill cannot take care of him by herself and she has to employ help. Nurses come to their home every day and provide the care Bill needs. Medical expenses begin to pile up, and Jill must draw more and more money from their savings. Their savings continues to dwindle, but Jill feels that she needs to spend whatever it costs to care for her husband in his last years.

Eventually Bill passes away, and even though Jill knew this day was going to come, emotionally it is still very difficult for her. Bill is gone; leaving a huge void in her life. They were together for so long that it is hard for Jill to remember what her life was like before Bill. Even though she has her children, they live far away in different cities and for the first time in her life, Jill feels alone.

The emotional toll of Bill's death is bad enough, but Jill has more bad news to deal with. The nest egg of savings that they had accumulated is almost completely gone. The majority of it was spent on Bill's medical expenses incurred during the last two years of his life.

When Bill was alive, they received two Social Security checks. Bill received the larger one and Jill received the smaller one. Now that Bill has died, Jill only gets one check. Luckily for Jill, she can still receive the bigger check, but her smaller check stops. At the end of the day, she has a reduction in her Social Security income of 40%.

Jill is still in relatively good health and could potentially live for many more years, even well into her 90s. She is going to have to survive on little or no savings and the smallest Survivor Benefit possible, because Bill claimed his Social Security benefits at age 62. Her comfortable retirement has become uncomfortable, and it may be difficult for her to make ends meet. She does not want to become a burden to their children, but she fears that is where she is headed.

Things could have been a lot different if Bill had delayed claiming his Social Security benefits as long as possible. Jill would have been provided with the largest Survivor Benefit possible, which would have left her in a much better financial position to maintain her quality of life after Bill's death. When Bill and Jill claimed their Social Security benefits at age 62, neither of them asked the question: "What happens when one of us dies?" They did not think about what life would be like for the surviving spouse. If they had, they may have made different decisions and delayed Bill's benefits as long as possible. Now, it's too late, and Jill is left alone to suffer the consequences.

THE SILENT CRISIS

The story of Bill and Jill is one example of why many women struggle after their husbands pass away, and why the rates of poverty for older widowed women are so much higher than the rates of poverty for older married women. Many American women are having, or have had, an experience similar to Jill's. Most often it is the wife who makes the sacrifices and compromises in their careers in the best interest of their children and family. This often negatively impacts their earnings history, and results in a smaller Social Security check. Usually, the husband ends up with the larger Social Security check and too often, a couple does not consider what will happen when one spouse passes away. There is a silent crisis of older, widowed women in the U.S. who struggle financially or live in poverty. Making the right Social Security claiming decision can play an important role in changing the outcome of the women who are affected by this crisis.

THE HIGHER-EARNING SPOUSE CAN LEAVE A SURVIVOR BENEFIT THAT IS TWO CHECKS IN ONE

Many married couples claim their Social Security benefits at age 62. Most older, married women do not struggle financially or live below the poverty line while their husbands are still living because they are receiving two Social Security checks. The surviving spouse would not struggle as much financially, if at all, after her husband dies, if he left her with a Survivor Benefit check that is just as big or even bigger than the combined total of the two checks they received when they were both living. If the couple could leave the survivor with the equivalent of TWO checks after the death of the first spouse (usually the husband), it could greatly reduce the probability that the wife will struggle financially after his death.

In Chapter 7, I showed you how, by making a better Social Security claiming decision, a married couple can achieve a Survivor Benefit check that is as big as TWO Checks In ONE. The table below shows you how you can do this.

TABLE 8.1

A	B	C	D	E	F
Bill's Claiming Age	Bill's Monthly Check at Age 82	** Jill's Monthly Check at Age 82	Bill and Jill's Total Combined Income [Two Checks B+C]	Monthly Survivor Benefit (Bill Dies at 82 yrs) [One Check]	Yearly Survivor Benefit (Bill Dies at 82 yrs)
62	$2,031	$1,354	$3,385	$2,235***	$26,820
70	$3,576	$1,354	$4,930	$3,576	$42,912

It's like TWO checks in ONE. ONE check of $3,576 (Survivor Benefit) in Column "E" is bigger than the combined total of $3,385 from TWO checks in Column "D".

*Assumed an annual COLA increase of 3.00%.

**Column "C" - Jill's smaller check will stop after Bill dies at age 82.

***Minimum Survivor Benefit when Bill claimed at age 62.

The number $3,385 circled in Column D represents the combined total of the TWO checks the couple would receive if they both claimed their benefits at age 62. The number $3,576 circled in Column E represents the size of the ONE Survivor Benefit check if the spouse with the bigger benefit, in this case Bill, claimed his benefit at age 70. The ONE Survivor Benefit check is bigger than the combined total of the TWO checks. That's how making a better Social Security claiming decision can provide a Survivor Benefit check that is as big as TWO checks in ONE, which should reduce the probability that the surviving spouse will struggle financially after the first spouse dies.

It doesn't work like this all the time. Sometimes when the spouse with the bigger benefit claims at age 70, it doesn't result in a Survivor Benefit that is as big as two checks in one. But in those cases, the Survivor Benefit is almost as big as two checks in one. Either way, making the Survivor Benefit as big as possible should make life easier for the surviving spouse after the first spouse dies.

ARE BILL AND JILL THE EXCEPTIONS...OR THE RULE?

You may be wondering how many couples have a similar experience to that of Bill and Jill. I do not have any hard numbers or statistics on how often married, retired couples have a life experience similar to that of Bill and Jill's, but I've done quite a bit of research on the topic, and it is my conclusion that some version of the Bill and Jill story is replayed quite often across the United States. My wife and I have lived a version of it. We are more than halfway through our version of the story, and so far, ours is very similar to that of Bill and Jill's. I am working very hard, however, to make sure that the ending is not the same for my wife. Our ending is going to be different because I am going to wait until I am 70 years old to claim my Social Security benefits and leave her with the largest Survivor Benefit possible.

ACKNOWLEDGING THE SILENT CRISIS

Too many single, older women struggle financially or live in poverty. This is a silent crisis because our society does not discuss it and, as a result, very few people acknowledge it. People making better Social Security claiming decisions could make a huge difference in reducing the size of this problem.

The time to act is the point when a couple is deciding when to retire and when they will claim their Social Security benefits. Making a better Social Security claiming decision could make a big difference in decreasing the chances that one of you will struggle financially after the first spouse dies. Mother Teresa said that "if you can't feed a hundred people, then feed just one". You can change the world if you can help make one person's life better.

Therefore, tell a friend about this silent crisis and let them know how their Social Security claiming decision can make a big difference in ensuring that they do not become part of it.

CHAPTER 8 IMPORTANT CONCEPTS:

• Many women struggle after their husbands pass away because, many times, the husband claims his larger Social Security benefit as early as possible, leaving his widowed wife with the smallest Survivor Benefit possible. That is one of the reasons why the rates of poverty for older widowed women are so much higher than the rates of poverty for older married women.

• When the higher-earning spouse delays his benefit claim until age 70, this often results in a Survivor Benefit check that is as big as TWO checks in ONE.

• The time to act is when a couple is deciding when to retire and when they will claim their Social Security benefits. Making a better Social Security claiming decision could make a big difference in decreasing the chances that one spouse will struggle financially after the first spouse dies.

• The best strategy for single women, who were never married, is to delay claiming their Social Security benefits as long as possible in order to maximize their Work History Benefit.

SOURCES:

1. Weiss, Liz, Unmarried Women Hit Hard by Poverty (Washington, DC: Center for American Progress, September 2009.)

2. Social Security Administration, The Retirement Prospects of Divorced Women (United States: SSA November 1, 2012)

3. Social Security Administration, Social Security is Important for Women (United States: SSA March 2014)

4. Social Security Administration, Social Security is Important for Women

5. United States Census 2010 (United States: US Census, 2010)

6. Social Security Administration, The Retirement Prospects of Divorced Women

WHY WAIT FACTOR #7
THE SPOUSAL BENEFIT

The Spousal Benefit is **the secret weapon** that most married couples can use to maximize their Social Security benefits. Millions of people currently receive their Social Security benefits in the form of a Spousal Benefit. Most of them claim their Spousal Benefit in the conventional way. I also recommend using the Spousal Benefit in an unconventional way, which can enable a married couple to substantially increase their Social Security benefits.

The Spousal Benefit is the driving force behind many of the Getting Paid To Wait claiming strategies. It is imperative to have a strong understanding of your secret weapon, the Spousal Benefit, because it is the key to the simple, powerful, Getting Paid To Wait strategies for married couples and divorced spouses.

THE CONVENTIONAL APPROACH TO CLAIMING THE SPOUSAL BENEFIT

A Spousal Benefit is paid to one spouse based on the Work History Benefit that the other spouse would receive at his or her Full Retirement Age. The maximum amount that a spouse can receive from a Spousal Benefit is 50% of the other spouse's Work History Benefit at Full Retirement Age.

Using our Cris and Lee example, if Cris, the higher-earning spouse, had a Work History Benefit of $2,000 per month at his Full Retirement Age, then Lee, the lower-earning spouse, would be entitled to receive a Spousal Benefit equal to 50% of that $2,000, or $1,000 per month. **Lee is entitled to receive 50% of Cris's Full Retirement Age Benefit only if Lee waits until his or her Full Retirement Age to claim the Spousal Benefit.** If Lee chooses to claim the Spousal Benefit before age 66, there will be a reduction of the benefit to less than 50%.

The earliest that a spouse can claim a Spousal Benefit is age 62. If claimed at age 62, the Spousal Benefit is reduced to 35% of the other spouse's Work History Benefit. If Lee claimed the Spousal Benefit at age 62 instead of age 66, the benefit will be reduced to only 35% of Cris's Work History Benefit of $2,000, or $700 per month. The maximum amount of the Spousal Benefit is the 50% that can be received if Lee claims at Full Retirement Age.

TABLE 9.1

Cris's Full Retirement Age Benefit - $2,000. Lee's Full Retirement Age Benefit - $500.

Age	62	63	64	65	66	67	68	69	70
Cris's Monthly Benefit	$0	$0	$0	$0	$2,000	$2,000	$2,000	$2,000	$2,000
Lee's Monthly Benefit	$0	$0	$0	$0	$1,000	$1,000	$1,000	$1,000	$1,000

Lee claims a Spousal Benefit of $1,000 per month at age 66.

When used in the conventional way, a spouse would claim a Spousal Benefit only if it was going to be larger than his or her own Work History Benefit. Table 9.1 shows you how this works. In this situation, Cris's Social Security Work History Benefit at Full Retirement Age is $2,000 per month and Lee's Full Retirement Age Work History Benefit is only $500 per month. Because Lee's benefit is so much smaller than Cris's benefit, Lee will receive more Social Security income by utilizing the Spousal Benefit.

In Table 9.1, the top row shows a range of ages starting at age 62 and ending with age 70. I have assumed both spouses are the same age. The second row shows the amount of the monthly Social Security check Cris receives at each different age. The last row shows the amount of the monthly Social Security check Lee receives. If both spouses wait until their Full Retirement Age of 66 to claim their benefits, Cris receives a Full Retirement Age Work History Benefit of $2,000 per month. When Lee claims a benefit at age 66, instead of receiving a Work History Benefit of only $500, because Lee is entitled to receive a Spousal Benefit, Lee's check is increased to $1,000 per month. In this case, the Spousal Benefit doubled the amount of Lee's monthly check from $500 per month, to $1,000 per month.

OVERVIEW OF THE SPOUSAL BENEFIT:

• The maximum amount a spouse can receive from a Spousal Benefit is 50% of the other spouse's Work History Benefit at Full Retirement Age.

• Once a married spouse has filed for his or her Work History Benefit, the other spouse can then claim a Spousal Benefit.

• It does not matter at what age the other spouse filed for his or her Work History Benefits. The amount of the Spousal Benefit will only be reduced if the spouse claiming the Spousal Benefit claims prior to his or her own Full Retirement Age.

• Many divorced spouses can also use the Spousal Benefit as their secret weapon to help maximize their Social Security benefits.

AND IT GETS EVEN BETTER

TABLE 9.2

Cris's Full Retirement Age Benefit - $2,000. Lee's Full Retirement Age Benefit - $500.									
Age	**62**	**63**	**64**	**65**	**66**	**67**	**68**	**69**	**70**
Cris's Monthly Benefit	$1,500	$1,500	$1,500	$1,500	$1,500	$1,500	$1,500	$1,500	$1,500
Lee's Monthly Benefit	$0	$0	$0	$0	$1,000	$1,000	$1,000	$1,000	$1,000

Cris claims his benefit at age 62 and it is reduced to only $1,500 per month (75% x $2,000 = $1,500)

Lee claims a Spousal Benefit and receives $1,000 per month which is 50% of Cris's Full Retirement Age Benefit of $2,000 (50% x $2,000 = $1,000)

The age at which Cris claims the Work History Benefit does not impact the amount of the Spousal Benefit that Lee is entitled to receive. Referring to Table 9.2, in this case, Cris decides to claim early at age 62 and receives a reduced benefit of $1,500 per month. Lee waits until age 66 to claim a benefit, and because Lee is entitled to a Spousal Benefit, she receives $1,000 per month, which is 50% of Cris's Full Retirement Age Benefit of $2,000. You may think that Lee would only receive $750 per month because, by Cris claiming the Work History Benefit at age 62, it was reduced from $2,000 to only $1,500, and 50% of $1,500 is $750. However, this is not the case. Because Lee waited until the Full Retirement Age of 66 to claim, Lee receives 50% of Cris's Full Retirement Age Work History Benefit, or 50% of $2,000, which equals $1,000. The fact that Cris's Work History Benefit was reduced to only $1,500 because it was claimed early at age 62 has no effect on the size of Lee's Spousal Benefit. The percentage of the Spousal Benefit is reduced only if the spouse filing for the Spousal Benefit is younger than Full Retirement Age at the time he or she makes the claim.

THE CONVENTIONAL APPROACH

When the Spousal Benefit is used in the conventional way, the spouse with the smaller Work History Benefit is the one who claims the Spousal Benefit. In Tables 9.1 and Table 9.2, using the Spousal Benefit in the conventional way increased Lee's Social Security income from $500 per month (Lee's own Work History Benefit) to $1,000 per month (Spousal Benefit). For many married couples, using the Spousal Benefit in the conventional way may be their best option to provide them with a larger amount of Social Security income.

The Spousal Benefit can generously provide a married couple with the means to increase their benefits. Even though one spouse in a married couple may have worked very little or not at all, he or she is still entitled to receive a substantial monthly Social Security check because of the Spousal Benefit. That alone makes the Spousal Benefit a great feature, and using it in the conventional way can be very beneficial to a married couple.

AN UNCONVENTIONAL APPROACH

The Bipartisan Budget Act of 2015 put new restrictions on using the Spousal Benefit in an unconventional way. Only people who were age 62 or older by December 31, 2015 can use the Spousal Benefit in the unconventional way that is explained in this section.

Instead of the spouse with the smaller Work History Benefit claiming a Spousal Benefit, when you use the Spousal Benefit in the unconventional way, it is the spouse with the larger Work History Benefit who claims the Spousal Benefit.

Why would the spouse with the larger Work History Benefit claim a Spousal Benefit? If Cris and Lee proceed this way, then Cris will receive a monthly Spousal Benefit check much smaller than the size of the check he or she would receive if Cris had claimed his or her own Work History Benefit. However, using this approach, Cris will receive the smaller Spousal Benefit check only for a short period of time.

USING THE SPOUSAL BENEFIT IN THE UNCONVENTIONAL WAY IS ONE OF THE KEYS TO THE GETTING PAID TO WAIT STRATEGIES.

After this short period of time, Cris will switch from the Spousal Benefit to his or her own unclaimed and even larger Work History Benefit. The entire time Cris was receiving the Spousal Benefit, Cris continued to delay claiming his or her own Work History Benefit and continued earning Delayed Retirement Credits. During this time, Cris's Work History Benefit grew by 8% for each additional year that claiming was delayed. Spousal Benefits enable married and many divorced couples to craft Social Security claiming strategies that pay them to wait and make it easier for them to greatly increase their Social Security income throughout their retirement lifetime.

Don't worry if it is still unclear how you can use the Spousal Benefit in the unconventional way to maximize your Social Security benefits. When we get to the Getting Paid To Wait Strategies in Chapters 12 and 13, you will see exactly how it works.

CHAPTER 9 IMPORTANT CONCEPTS:

• The Spousal Benefit is the driving force behind the Getting Paid To Wait claiming strategies.

• The maximum amount that a spouse can receive from a Spousal Benefit is 50% of the other spouse's Work History Benefit at Full Retirement Age.

• When the Spousal Benefit is used in the conventional way, the spouse with the smaller Work History Benefit is the one who claims the Spousal Benefit.

• Instead of the spouse with the smaller Work History Benefit claiming a Spousal Benefit, using the Spousal Benefit in the unconventional way, it is the spouse with the larger Work History Benefit who claims the Spousal Benefit for a limited period of time.

WHY WAIT FACTOR #8
THE WORKING LONGER BENEFIT

TRY TO REMOVE THE EMOTIONAL ELEMENT OF WORKING PAST AGE 62

Working even a few more years can make a big difference in how financially comfortable you are in your retirement. The average retirement age in this country is rising, which is also resulting in more people delaying the claiming of their Social Security benefits.[1] In 2012, the average age that people claimed their Social Security benefits was the oldest it had been in over 30 years.[2] I would like to think that one of the reasons why so many more people are working longer is so that they can delay claiming their Social Security benefits.

The current trend is to work longer, and it appears that many people are perfectly happy working a few more years in their current job. At age 62, most people are still very vibrant and energetic. Their experience in their industry will be difficult to replace and they are valued members of the workforce in their current position. Continuing in your current role may allow you to earn at your highest income level yet. Some people love their jobs! If you are one of those people, keep working. If you don't love your job, consider sticking it out for a few more years, or even cutting back your hours and working part-time. It is in your best interest to continue to work and earn a good income, which will deliver benefits down the road that you may not have considered.

If you have already made up your mind to retire early and claim your Social Security benefits at age 62, it may be an emotional challenge to change your mind and work a few more years. This aspect of your retirement decision can be a difficult obstacle to overcome.

By removing the emotional element from the decision, you can evaluate the financial impact of retirement based on numbers and math. Whether or not you have accumulated savings, working a few more years can have a huge impact on your quality of life in retirement.

DID A GREAT IDEA BACKFIRE?

In 1956, the United States Government lowered the earliest age at which women could claim their Social Security benefits from age 65 to age 62.[3] Before 1956, the earliest a woman could claim Social Security benefits was age 65. At that time, on average, the husband was approximately three years older than the wife.[4] If the husband retired and claimed his Social Security benefits at age 65, his wife, only age 62, had to work three more years before she could retire and collect her benefits, at age 65.

The government had good intentions when it lowered the earliest claiming age for women to age 62. The reasoning behind the change was to allow the average husband and wife to retire at the same time—the husband could retire at 65, his wife could retire when she was age 62, and both could claim their Social Security benefits during the same year. In 1961, the government also lowered the earliest age in which a man could claim Social Security benefits to age 62.[5]

This rule change for both men and women effectively lowered the average retirement age in the United States, which also coincided with an increasing life expectancy in this country. People were retiring earlier and living longer. These factors made the demands on the Social Security system greater and the financial challenges retirees face even larger. The trend persists today. Even though the average retirement age has become slightly older in the last few years, it is still relatively young, and life expectancy continues to increase.[6]

MAKING THE MONEY LAST

A major concern for most retirees is maintaining their quality of life for as long as they live. Ideally, they want to be able to pay all their bills and have money left over to have some fun—travel, entertainment, charity work, or hobbies. Retirees who are fortunate enough to have some savings are concerned about making those savings last as long as they do. They fear a situation in which their savings are depleted at age 80, but they are still alive at age 85, 90, or even 100. They do not want to run out of money before they run out of breath. Retirees who have little or no accumulated savings may worry about struggling to make ends meet throughout their retirement, especially in their later years when their options are limited.

There is a simple solution that can make these issues less of a challenge: work longer! If you can, a number of great things can happen.

IS YOUR PLAN SUSTAINABLE FOR 25 OR 30 YEARS?

Many people assess their financial situation when they are nearing age 62 to decide when and if they can afford to retire. The couple considers the income they will receive from Social Security, as well as any additional income or savings they have accumulated. Emotions can play a big part in their decision. They want to retire and do not always look at their situation realistically. Even though they may just barely be able to make ends meet, they plan on spending less when they retire and believe they will be able to survive financially.

Frequently, these early retirees do not fully appreciate the financial challenges that living 20 or 30 years in retirement may present. They do not fully consider what retirement may look like at different points during their future—at age 70, 75, 80, 85, and beyond. They do not realize that just because they can make ends meet while they are in their early 60s, does not necessarily mean this will be the case when they are in their mid-70s or early 80s. They are not factoring in the effects of the retirement income threats and the threat magnifier:

- Inflation

- Unplanned medical expenses

- Investment ups and downs

- Withdrawing too much, too soon from savings (2much2soon)

- Longevity—the threat magnifier

Most Americans, regardless of their financial situation in their early 60s, would be in a better position to handle the financial challenges they will face in retirement if they held off and claimed Social Security at their Full Retirement Age of 66, or even better, at age 70. Working three or four more years can make it easier to delay claiming Social Security benefits, which can significantly impact your quality of life, especially in the later years of retirement.

7 WAIT FACTOR BONUSES ARE TRIGGERED
IF YOU WORK A LITTLE LONGER

If you can delay claiming your benefits and properly execute the Getting Paid To Wait strategies, you will earn Wait Factor Bonuses:

Wait Factor Bonus #1: Higher-earning years are added to your Social Security calculations and lower-earning years are eliminated.

Wait Factor Bonus #2: Social Security income is higher when you work longer and claim your benefits later, leading to higher annual dollar increases because of COLA and a higher Survivor Benefit.

Wait Factor Bonus #3: When your Social Security income makes up a larger percentage of your retirement income, the amount you will need to withdraw from your savings decreases.

Wait Factor Bonus #4: You can save more, which results in a larger nest egg of savings when you retire.

Wait Factor Bonus #5: You will reduce the number of years your savings needs to last.

Wait Factor Bonus #6: The Compound Effect—Greater Social Security income (Bonus #1 & #2) results in lesser amounts withdrawn (Bonus #3) from a larger amount of savings (Bonus #4) and a shorter length of time accumulated savings must last (Bonus #5).

Wait Factor Bonus #7: If Social Security makes up a higher percentage of your retirement income, it could result in meaningful tax savings.

Wait Factor Bonus #1: Higher-earning years are added to your Social Security calculations and lower-earning years are eliminated.

In determining the size of your Social Security benefit check, the Social Security Administration will look at your entire work history and pick your highest-paying or highest-earning 35 years. If we assume that you retire and claim your Social Security benefits at age 62, and every year you worked you made more money than the previous year, the Social Security Administration will look back to when you were 27 years old and use your highest 35 years of work history. To arrive at the starting point of age 27, we subtract 35 years from age 62 (62 - 35 = 27). If you have a year prior to age 27 when you earned more money than in any one of the 35 years from age 27 forward, the Social Security Administration will use that higher-earning year and drop the lowest-earning year between ages 27 and 62.

If you decide to work an additional four years until you reach your Full Retirement Age of 66, using the same assumptions, the Social Security Administration will look at your work history going back 35 years and start at age 31 (66 - 35 = 31).

In this case, by working four additional years, the Social Security Administration will drop off your earning years of 27, 28, 29, and 30 and add on your earning years of 63, 64, 65, and 66 years old. Most people earn more money later in their career than early on. Therefore, by working an additional four years, the lowest-earning years (ages 27, 28, 29, and 30) are dropped from the Social Security calculation and four higher-earning years (63, 64, 65, and 66) are added in, which should result in a higher monthly Social Security check.

CASE STUDY: SANDY'S EARNING HISTORY

TABLE 10.1

A	B	C	D	
Age	Earnings	Retire at Age 62	Retire at Age 66	
27	$30,000	$30,000		
28	$30,900	$30,900		These 4 yrs of earnings drop off.
29	$31,827	$31,827		
30	$32,781	$32,781		
31	$33,765	$33,765	$33,765	
32	$34,778	$34,778	$34,778	
33	$35,821	$35,821	$35,821	
34	$36,896	$36,896	$36,896	
35	$38,003	$38,003	$38,003	
36	$39,143	$39,143	$39,143	
37	$40,317	$40,317	$40,317	
38	$41,527	$41,527	$41,527	
39	$42,772	$42,772	$42,772	
40	$44,056	$44,056	$44,056	
41	$45,377	$45,377	$45,377	
42	$46,739	$46,739	$46,739	
43	$48,141	$48,141	$48,141	
44	$49,585	$49,585	$49,585	
45	$51,072	$51,072	$51,072	
46	$52,605	$52,605	$52,605	
47	$54,183	$54,183	$54,183	
48	$55,808	$55,808	$55,808	
49	$57,403	$57,403	$57,403	
50	$59,207	$59,207	$59,207	
51	$60,983	$60,983	$60,983	
52	$62,813	$62,813	$62,813	
53	$64,697	$64,697	$64,697	
54	$66,638	$66,638	$66,638	
55	$68,637	$68,637	$68,637	
56	$70,686	$70,686	$70,686	
57	$72,817	$72,817	$72,817	
58	$75,002	$75,002	$75,002	
59	$77,252	$77,252	$77,252	
60	$79,570	$79,570	$79,570	
61	$81,957	$81,957	$81,957	
62	$84,415	$84,415	$84,415	
63	$86,948		$86,948	
64	$89,556		$89,556	These 4 yrs of earnings are added on.
65	$92,243		$92,243	
66	$95,010		$95,010	

Looking at Table 10.1, Column B shows the earnings for each year of Sandy's working life. At age 27, Sandy earned $30,000. For purposes of this example, I assumed that every year her earnings increased by 3%, up to age 66, when she earned $95,010. Column C looks at the earnings history if Sandy retired at age 62. In order to determine the size of her monthly check, the Social Security Administration would use the prior 35 years of earnings history, which would take them all the way back to age 27. Column D shows Sandy's earnings history if she retired at age 66. The Social Security Administration would look at her earnings history, going back to age 31. You can see the difference that working four more years can make. By working until age 66, the low-earning years when Sandy was age 27 ($30,000), 28 ($30,900), 29 ($31,827), and 30 ($32,781) are dropped and her highest wage-earning years of age 63 ($84,415), 64 ($89,556), 65 ($92,243), and 66 ($95,010) are added in.

Working four more years can result in a larger monthly Social Security check. It may not be substantially larger because you only change four out of the 35 years and Social Security does use a weighted average formula that increases the value of your early-earning years. In general, however, your check should be larger and that is a major benefit.

Wait Factor Bonus #2: Social Security income is higher when you work longer and claim your benefits later, leading to higher annual dollar increases because of COLA and a higher Survivor Benefit.

Claiming your benefits at your Full Retirement Age of 66 will result in a check that is 33% larger than the check you would receive if you claimed at age 62. A bigger Social Security check means bigger annual increases because of COLA. It also results in a larger Survivor Benefit. And the numbers are even better if you wait until age 70 to claim your benefits.

> These first two Wait Factor Bonuses apply to everyone. The next few Wait Factor Bonuses apply to people who have some accumulated savings in addition to their Social Security income.

Wait Factor Bonus #3: When your Social Security income makes up a larger percentage of your retirement income, the amount you will need to withdraw from your savings decreases.

If your Social Security income is not going to be enough to cover your retirement living expenses, you will be required to withdraw money from your accumulated savings. We discussed earlier that withdrawing too much, too soon (2much2soon) from your savings was one of the retirement income threats magnified by longevity (See also, Chapter 3). The less you have to withdraw from savings, the longer your savings will last. If your Social Security check is larger, because you delayed claiming, you will not have to withdraw as much from your savings and, consequently, your savings should last longer. The goal should be to make your savings last as long as you live. Working a few more years could greatly increase the odds of that happening.

CASE STUDY: CASEY AND ALEX FACE THE 2MUCH2SOON THREAT

TABLE 10.2

	Age 62	Age 66
A) Monthly Income Needed	$3,000	$3,000
B) Monthly Income from Social Security	$2,000	$2,660
C) Monthly Shortfall (Row A - Row B)	$1,000	$340
D) Annual Shortfall (Amount withdrawn from Savings) (Row C x 12)	$12,000	$4,080

Casey and Alex need to withdraw money from their savings because their Social Security income isn't enough to pay all of their bills, which total $3,000 per month. Table 10.2 illustrates the difference in claiming Social Security benefits at age 62 or age 66, and the effect it has on how much money needs to be withdrawn from their savings. Line A in the table, indicates that Casey and Alex have a monthly income need of $3,000 and this amount is the same at age 62 or age 66.

Line B shows that if Casey and Alex claim their Social Security at age 62, they receive $2,000 per month, but if they wait until age 66, their benefits are 33% bigger and they receive $2,660 per month. Line C shows the amount of money that must be withdrawn every month from savings in order to pay the bills. Claiming their Social Security benefits at age 62 will result in a $1,000 ($3,000 - $2,000) shortfall every month. Claiming benefits at age 66 reduces the monthly shortfall to only $340 ($3,000 - $2,660).

Line D shows the total amount of money that must be withdrawn that year from their savings in order to pay their bills. If Casey and Alex claim their Social Security benefits at age 62, they will have an annual shortfall of $12,000, which is the amount they will need to withdraw from their savings. If they wait and claim their benefits at age 66, their monthly shortfall is only $340, resulting in an annual shortfall of $4,080. This allows them to reduce the amount they must withdraw from their savings. Table 10.2 illustrates that withdrawing only $4,080 instead of $12,000 every year from their savings, should make their savings last a lot longer.

Working four more years, from age 62 to age 66, will allow you to delay claiming your benefits until age 66, which increases your Social Security income and reduces the amount of money you need to withdraw from your savings. The goal is to make your savings last as long as you live. Working a few more years could greatly increase the odds of that happening.

Wait Factor Bonus #4: You can save more, which results in a larger nest egg of savings when you retire.

Retiring with accumulated savings is a great accomplishment and the more savings you have, the better. If you work until age 66 instead of retiring at age 62, those four additional years provide an opportunity to add to your savings. Hopefully, by age 62, most of your major expenses have disappeared or have been greatly reduced. Your children's education has been paid for and your home mortgage is paid off. For most people, the years between 62 and 66, are high-earning years. If your living expenses are lower and your earnings are higher, you should be in a great position to save money during the four additional years (age 62 to age 66) that you choose to work.

CASE STUDY: CASEY AND ALEX DECIDE
TO CONTINUE WORKING

TABLE 10.3

A	B*	C
Age	Retire at 62 Savings	Retire at 66 Savings
62	$200,000	$200,000
63	$188,000	$225,000
64	$176,000	$250,000
65	$164,000	$275,000
66	$152,000	$300,000
* When they retire at age 62 they withdraw $12,000 every year.		

Increasing your accumulated savings, whether by a large amount or a small amount, is a good thing. Table 10.3 shows you the potential effect that working four more years could have on the size of your savings account. Casey and Alex could retire at age 62 with $200,000 in accumulated savings, as shown in Column B, or they could work four more years and retire at age 66 with $300,000 in accumulated savings, as shown in Column C. Their savings grew to $300,000 in Column C because each additional year that they worked they were able to save $25,000. Over the four-year period during which they continued to work, they were able to save an additional $100,000, which increased their total savings from $200,000 at age 62 to $300,000 at age 66.

In Column B, when Casey and Alex retired at age 62, they started out with total savings of $200,000, but four years later, at age 66, their savings had decreased to $152,000. This happened because, as we saw in Table 10.2, when they retired at age 62, they needed to withdraw $12,000 every year from their savings in order to pay all of their bills. Every year over the four-year period from age 62 to age 66, their savings decreased by $12,000, or a total of $48,000 ($12,000 x 4). Not only do they need to withdraw a larger amount of money from a smaller amount of savings, but they also have to do it over a longer period of time because they retired at age 62 instead of age 66.

If you work four more years and you are able to save more money over those four years, your nest egg, or retirement savings, will grow even larger. In this case, from $200,000 to $300,000. Even if you think that $25,000 of annual savings is an unrealistic number, but you can still manage $5,000 or $10,000, the concept still works. If you can increase your savings, you will end up withdrawing an even smaller percentage of money from your savings because your Social Security check is also bigger.

Wait Factor Bonus #5: You will reduce the number of years your savings needs to last.

In order to illustrate this Wait Factor Bonus, we need to make an assumption about the day you die—a thought many people consider unpleasant. If we assume your date of death does not change, regardless of when you begin your Social Security benefits, at age 62, 66, or 70, then the longer you work and delay Social Security, the shorter time period your savings will need to last.

CASE STUDY: GERRY LIVES TO 92

It would be nice to know how long you are going to live in retirement—is it going to be 10 years, 20 years, 30 years, or even 35–40 years? It would be easier to make your savings last as long as you live if you knew you were only going to live for 10 years, as opposed to 20 years; or 20 years as opposed to 30 years in retirement. But none of us have a crystal ball. The point is, the shorter the period of time, the easier it is to make your savings last. Or, the longer the period of time, the more difficult it becomes to make your savings last.

TABLE 10.4

	A	B	C
A) Assumed Age of Death	92	92	92
B) Retirement Age	62	66	70
C) Number of Years Saving Must Last (Row A - Row B)	(30 yrs)	(26 yrs)	(22 yrs)

Let's assume Gerry will live a long life and will die when he is 92 years old. Table 10.4 shows how long his savings must last if he retires at different ages. In Column A, if Gerry retired at age 62, his savings must last for 30 years in his retirement (92 - 62 = 30 years). Column B shows that if Gerry retired at age 66, his savings need to last only 26 years (92 - 66 = 26 years). Column C illustrates that if Gerry retired at age 70, then his savings would need to last for an even shorter period—just 22 years (92 - 70 = 22 years).

If you shorten the period of time your savings have to last, it becomes much easier to manage your finances during retirement. Each additional year you work is an additional year that you delay taking income from your savings. Returning to Casey and Alex, when they retired and claimed Social Security at age 62, they needed to withdraw money from savings at age 62. Table 10.3 shows that when Casey and Alex retired, they began withdrawing $12,000 every year to pay their bills. Retiring at age 66 delayed withdrawing money from savings by four years, which decreased the amount of time their savings had to last. Even working for just four more years, from age 62 to age 66, can have a significant impact of increasing the probability that your savings will last throughout your retirement, or for as long as you live.

Wait Factor Bonus #6: The Compound Effect—Greater Social Security income (Bonus #1 & #2) results in lesser amounts withdrawn (Bonus #3) from a larger amount of savings (Bonus #4) and a shorter length of time accumulated savings must last (Bonus #5).

Each one of these Wait Factor Bonuses taken individually would have a positive effect on your retirement security. However, when all of the Wait Factor Bonuses are combined, there is a very powerful compound effect created by the chain reaction that takes place by working a few more years. All of these Wait Factor Bonuses add up to a much higher probability that your savings will last as long as you do!

CASE STUDY: THE COMPOUND EFFECT OF THE WAIT FACTOR BONUSES FOR CASEY AND ALEX

THESE ARE THE ASSUMPTIONS THAT ARE MADE IN TABLE 10.5:

• Casey and Alex have a retirement income need of $3,000 per month—this is the amount required to cover their monthly living expenses.

• Social Security income of $2,000 per month, when claimed at age 62, or $2,660 per month if claimed at age 66. If they delay claiming Social Security until age 66, their income increases by 33%.

• Accumulated savings of $200,000 if Casey and Alex retire and claim Social Security at age 62.

• Accumulated savings of $300,000 if they retire and claim Social Security at age 66. Savings increased from working four more years and saving an additional $25,000 per year, or an additional $100,000 over that four-year period.

TABLE 10.5

		A	B
	Age	62	66
A) Monthly Income Needed		$3,000	$3,000
B) Monthly Income from Social Security		$2,000	$2,660
C) Monthly Shortfall (Row A - Row B)		$1,000	$340
D) Total Amount Withdrawn from Savings Every Year (Row C x 12)		$12,000*	$4,080**
E) Total Savings		$200,000	$300,000

* At age 62 - Start withdrawing $12,000 every year from savings of $200,000.

** At age 66 - Start withdrawing $4,080 every year from savings of $300,000.

Referencing Table 10.5, this chart illustrates the impact of a decision by Casey and Alex to work four more years, then retire and claim their Social Security at age 66. They have a Monthly Required Income need of $3,000. Line B shows the difference in their Monthly Income from Social Security if they work four more years. Lines C and D illustrate the difference in the amount of the Monthly Shortfall and the annual Amount Withdrawn from Savings. Because Casey and Alex worked these four additional years, they were able to save an additional $100,000, increasing their Total Savings (Line E) to $300,000. Starting at age 66, they were going to have to withdraw $4,080 per year from their increased total savings of $300,000.

By working four more years, Casey and Alex increased their Social Security income from $2,000 per month, to $2,660 per month (Bonus #1 and #2). By increasing their Social Security income, it reduced the annual amount they had to withdraw from their accumulated savings to $4,080, instead of $12,000 (Bonus #3). Their accumulated savings grew to $300,000 because, over the four additional working years, they saved $25,000 per year for a total of $100,000 in additional savings (Bonus #4). Because they didn't have to start withdrawing from their accumulated savings until age 66, those savings don't have to last as long—four years less than if they started to withdraw from their savings at age 62 (Bonus #5). Working four more years greatly improved the chances that their accumulated savings will last as long as Casey and Alex live.

Even if you think it's an unrealistic assumption that the accumulated savings would increase by $25,000 per year ($100,000) over those four additional work years, they are still much better off. Even if Casey and Alex didn't save any money over that four-year period and their accumulated savings stayed at $200,000, they still reduced the amount they needed to withdraw from savings and withdrew a smaller amount four years later, at age 66. Because they worked longer, they reduced the pressure on their savings by reducing the amount of money they needed to withdraw. Depending on how you invest your savings, lowering the amount you withdraw increases the likelihood that your savings could actually grow in your retirement!

Wait Factor Bonus #7: If Social Security makes up a higher percentage of your retirement income, it could result in meaningful tax savings.

We saw how working longer and delaying your Social Security benefits will result in a bigger monthly Social Security check. Did you know that if your Social Security makes up a higher percentage of your retirement income, you could reduce the amount of taxes you have to pay? It is pretty amazing and I show you how this works in the next chapter.

IT DOESN'T MATTER IF YOU DON'T HAVE ANY SAVINGS

If a person has very little savings, or none at all, Social Security is going to be his or her only source of income in retirement. If you have very little or no savings, it is even more important for you to delay claiming your Social Security benefits as long as possible, so your check will be as large as possible. A larger Social Security check will help to make your retirement more comfortable. One of the best ways to make it easier for you to delay claiming your Social Security benefits and make your Social Security check bigger is to WORK LONGER!

CHAPTER 10 IMPORTANT CONCEPTS:

• One of the best ways to make it easier for you to delay claiming your Social Security benefits and make your Social Security check bigger is to WORK LONGER!

• Many people are choosing to work longer and retire later. This may be one of the reasons people are delaying the claiming of their Social Security benefits.

• Delaying the claiming of your Social Security benefits can trigger seven Wait Factor Bonuses that are likely to have a significant positive impact on your financial security during retirement.

• Working three or four more years can make it easier to delay claiming Social Security benefits, which can significantly impact your quality of life, especially in the later years of retirement.

• If you shorten the period of time your savings must last, it becomes easier to manage your finances during retirement. Each additional year you work is an additional year that you delay taking income from your savings.

SOURCES:

1. Riffkin, Rebecca, Average U.S. Retirement Age Rises to 62 (United States: GALLUP, April 28, 2014)

2. Social Security Administration, Annual Statistical Supplement (Washington, DC: SSA, 2013)

3. Congressional Budget Office, Raising the Ages of Eligibility for Medicare and Social Security (Washington, DC: CBO, January 2012)

4. U.S. Census Bureau, Median Age at First Marriage by Sex 1890-2010 (United States: U.S. Census Bureau)

5. Congressional Budget Office, Raising the Ages of Eligibility for Medicare and Social Security (Washington, DC: CBO, January 2012)

6. Riffkin, Rebecca, Average U.S. Retirement Age Rises to 62 (United States: GALLUP, April 28, 2014)

WHY WAIT FACTOR #9
THE TAX BENEFIT

Increasing your Social Security income could decrease the amount of taxes you have to pay. If Social Security is only a part of your retirement income, or you have other sources of income (savings or investments) in addition to your Social Security income, increasing the percentage that comes from Social Security benefits could potentially decrease the amount you pay in income taxes.

Social Security income is reported to the IRS in a unique way. A special worksheet is used, and only 50% of your Social Security income is used in the calculation to determine how much of it is taxable. This has the potential to give your Social Security income huge tax advantages over your savings and investment income.

IF YOU INCREASE THE PERCENTAGE OF YOUR RETIREMENT INCOME THAT YOU RECEIVE FROM SOCIAL SECURITY BENEFITS, YOU COULD REDUCE THE AMOUNT OF TAXES YOU PAY THE FEDERAL GOVERNMENT.

If Social Security is your only source of income in retirement, then you probably won't have to pay any taxes. If that is the case, the information in this chapter will not apply to your situation, but I think you will still find the information very interesting.

HOW TO MAKE YOUR SOCIAL SECURITY INCOME WORK FOR YOU

Assuming the amount of income you need in retirement is fairly constant, the best way to increase the percentage of your income that comes from Social Security is to delay claiming so your Social Security check is larger. This will also reduce the amount of the periodic withdrawals you need to make from your savings or investments, which should help make your savings and investments last longer.

CASE STUDY: CASEY AND ALEX ANALYZE WHAT THEY WOULD OWE IN TAXES

Working with a tax preparation specialist, I have prepared three scenarios that examine the potential tax liability of Social Security income when benefits are claimed at age 62, 66, and 70.

Casey and Alex are a married couple and they are both the same age. They need $60,000 of annual income during retirement. This amount is a constant, regardless of when they claim their benefits. It will cover all of their daily living expenses and allow them to also have some fun during their retirement. If their Social Security income is not sufficient to meet their annual income requirement of $60,000, the shortfall will be made up by withdrawing money from their savings and other investments.

The longer Casey and Alex delay claiming their Social Security benefits, the larger their Social Security checks will be and the less money they will need to withdraw from their savings and other investments. Depending on when Casey and Alex claim their Social Security benefits, the percentage of their total income requirement of $60,000, derived from Social Security, will change. Let's examine what happens to Casey and Alex's tax liability when they claim their Social Security benefits at ages 62, 66, and 70.

TABLE 11.1

A	B	C	D
Age	Social Security Income	Withdrawal from IRA	Annual Income
62	$27,000	$33,000	$60,000
66	$36,000	$24,000	$60,000
70	$47,520	$12,480	$60,000

Table 11.1 recaps the three different scenarios. Column A shows three different claiming ages. In Column B, you see the annual amount of Social Security income they will receive if they claim at that corresponding age. The numbers in Column C represent the amount of money that has to be withdrawn from their savings to meet their annual income need of $60,000, in Column D. I have assumed that the amount withdrawn from their savings came from an Individual Retirement Account or IRA. (I have used a married couple in this example, but you do not have to be married to take advantage of these potential tax savings.)

When Casey and Alex both claim at age 62, they receive the smallest amount of Social Security income—$27,000 annually (Column B). The shortfall of $33,000 (Column C) represents the amount of annual income that has to be withdrawn from their savings and other investments, in this case their IRA account, in order to meet their annual income requirement of $60,000 (Column D).

If Casey and Alex both claim at age 66, the amount of the annual Social Security income in Column B will increase to $36,000. By increasing their Social Security income, they also decreased the amount that they had to withdraw from their IRA, in Column C, to $24,000 ($60,000 - $36,000).

Delaying until age 70 maximizes their annual Social Security income to $47,520. As a result of maximizing their Social Security income, they have to withdraw even less from their IRA, only $12,480 ($60,000 - $47,520), in order to meet their annual income requirement of $60,000.

TABLE 11.2

		A	B	C
	Income	Age 62	Age 66	Age 70
1	Total Social Security Benefits	$27,000	$36,000	$47,520
2	Taxable IRA Distributions	$33,000	$24,000	$12,480
3	Taxable Social Security Benefits	$8,125	$5,000	$2,120
4	Adjusted Gross Income (1+3)	$41,125	$29,000	$14,600
5	TOTAL TAX	$2,529	$813	$0

Table 11.2 shows the abbreviated tax returns for Casey and Alex at the three different ages: 62 (Column A), 66 (Column B), and 70 (Column C). Their total income remains the same. However, when their Social Security income went up and their withdrawals from their IRA went down, their taxes decreased.

MORE SOCIAL SECURITY INCOME, SMALLER WITHDRAWLS AND LESS TAX OWED

Assuming that both Casey and Alex claim their benefits at age 62, on Line 1 it shows Total Social Security Benefits of $27,000. Line 2 indicates they withdrew $33,000 from their IRA. Even though Casey and Alex received $27,000 in Social Security income, after going through the special calculation to determine the taxable portion, it turns out that only $8,125 of it is taxable, as shown on Line 3. In this scenario, if they both claimed their Social Security benefits at age 62, on Line 5 you can see that they would have to pay $2,529 in taxes.

Assuming that both Casey and Alex claim Social Security benefits at age 66 in Column B, on Line 1 you see that their Total Social Security Benefits increase to $36,000. That decreases the amount they have to withdraw from their IRA to only $24,000 on Line 2. Even though their Social Security income increased from $27,000 (claimed at 62) to $36,000, their Taxable Social Security Benefits on Line 3 are reduced to $5,000.

You would think just the opposite would happen—as Social Security income is increased, more of it would become taxable, not less. However, this is not the case. As their Social Security income increased, even less of it was taxable. As a result, their Total Tax on Line 5 was also reduced to only $813. When they both claimed at age 62, on Line 5, you see they pay a Total Tax of $2,529. When they both claimed at age 66, they increased their total Social Security income and decreased their taxes to only $813. That's a tax savings of $1,716.

Column C assumes that both Casey and Alex claim their Social Security benefits at age 70. In this case, on Line 1, their Total Social Security Benefits are maxed out at $47,520. That further reduces the amount they have to withdraw from their IRA to only $12,480 on Line 2. By waiting to claim until age 70, Casey and Alex received the largest amount of Social Security income possible. Because they increased their Social Security income, they further decreased the amount of money they had to withdraw from their IRAs. Their Social Security income totals $47,520, but amazingly, on Line 3, their Taxable Social Security Benefits are a mere $2,120. It happened again! Their Social Security income increased, but even less of it was taxable. Going right to the bottom line you see that their Total Tax, on Line 5, is zero ($0).

DELAYING BENEFITS UNTIL AGE 70, ZERO OWED IN TAXES!

In all three of the situations we just reviewed, Casey and Alex's total income remained the same at $60,000. If you can replace more of the taxable income you take from your savings and investments with Social Security income, the amount you pay in taxes could be reduced or, in some situations, even eliminated. You accomplish this by delaying the claiming of your Social Security benefits as long as possible. When you do this, you will increase your Social Security income and reduce the amount you need to withdraw from your savings and investments. I am not saying that if you delay claiming your Social Security Benefits until age 70 that you will eliminate all of your tax liability, however, that is the way it worked out for Casey and Alex. What I am saying is: if you replace some of the income you receive from your savings with income from Social Security, it could reduce the amount of taxes you have to pay.

Go through these same scenarios using your own Social Security claiming information. You could do the calculations yourself or employ the services of a tax preparer and ask him or her to prepare different tax calculations for you, assuming different ages of Social Security claiming and the associated income. Ask the tax preparer to determine what amount of taxes you will have to pay if you claim your Social Security benefits at age 62, 66, 70, or any age in-between. It is important that you first determine the level of total annual income that you will need in your retirement.

If your retirement income is less than $100,000 per year, and if you plan on taking money from your retirement accounts (IRAs, 401(k)s, etc.) or savings accounts as a source of additional income in your retirement, this exercise could prove to be extremely valuable in that you may be able to reduce the amount of taxes you pay each year in your retirement. If you do not have any savings, and Social Security is going to be your only source of income in your retirement, then you most likely will not have to pay any taxes and do not need to go through this exercise. If you are fortunate enough to have a very high level of income in your retirement, then this strategy may not be able to significantly reduce your taxes.

ADDITIONAL READING

James Mahaney and Peter C. Carlson authored a research paper entitled "Rethinking Social Security Claiming in a 401(k) World", which appeared in the book *Recalibrating Retirement Spending and Saving*. I first became aware of the tax benefits of Social Security income when I read their research paper. I found much of the information shared in their research paper to be both unique and incredible, and it changed the way I looked at Social Security income.

CHAPTER 11 IMPORTANT CONCEPTS:

• If you increase the percentage of your retirement income that you receive from Social Security benefits, you could reduce the amount of taxes you pay the federal government.

• If you do not have any savings, and Social Security is going to be your only source of income in your retirement, then you most likely will not have to pay any taxes and do not need to go through this exercise.

• If you are fortunate enough to have a very high level of income in your retirement, then this strategy may not be able to significantly reduce your taxes.

SOURCES

1. Mahaney, James and Carlson, Peter, *Rethinking Social Security Claiming in a 401(k) World* (Philadelphia, PA: University of Pennsylvania, August 2007)

PART III
THE
GETTING
PAID TO WAIT
STRATEGIES

CLAIM EARLY, CLAIM LATE
(RESTRICTED APPLICATION)

MAKING THE CLAIMING DECISION SIMPLE AND EASY

If you are age 62 or older before January 1, 2016, you are still eligible or qualified to use the Claim Early, Claim Late (Restricted Application) strategy explained and illustrated in this chapter. You don't have to use or implement the strategy before that date. If you are age 62 before January 1, 2016 you are "Grandfathered" and can still use the strategy after that date.

To help you determine if you are qualified to use this Claim Early, Claim Late (Restricted Application) strategy, please visit my website at www. gettingpaidtowait.com and use my Paid to Wait Social Security Calculator. The Paid to Wait Social Security Calculator will tell you if you are qualified to use the strategy and then will show exactly how it would work in your personal situation.

Because it has over 2,800 rules, many people think that Social Security is very complicated. I hope to help make your Social Security claiming decision both simple and easy. I will make it simple because I think almost every married couple should have the same primary goal of maximizing the higher-earning spouse's Social Security benefit. In other words, the spouse with the bigger benefit should delay claiming as long as possible so his or her Social Security check will be as big as possible. I hope to make it easy for you to do that by showing you the one claiming strategy that will pay you the most amount of Social Security income while the spouse with the bigger benefit delays claiming it.

IT WORKS FOR MANY PEOPLE

The Claim Early, Claim Late strategy is one of those strategies and provides a way for a qualified married couple to receive some income from Social Security while they delay. In many situations, the amount of Social Security income the couple receives while they are delaying can be quite substantial. Think of it as Getting Paid To Wait. The key to this strategy is the unconventional way it utilizes a married couple's secret weapon: the Spousal Benefit.

Many qualified married couples can use this strategy because it does not require you to have a large amount of accumulated savings in order to use it. In fact, it is probably more important for qualified married couples to use this strategy if they haven't saved any or very little and will be critically or totally dependent on Social Security for their retirement income.

If you have money saved, choosing the Claim Early, Claim Late strategy could greatly increase the probability that your accumulated savings will last as long as you do. If one of your biggest concerns is making sure that you don't run out of money before you run out of breath, then using the Claim Early, Claim Late strategy could be one of the best things you could do to increase your financial security during your retirement years.

THE CLAIM EARLY, CLAIM LATE STRATEGY

- The goal is to maximize the size of the higher-earner's Social Security benefit check and pay them the most amount of money while they wait.
- The lower-earning spouse (with the smaller Work History Benefit) claims at age 62.
- The higher-earning spouse claims and restricts his or her benefit to only a Spousal Benefit at Full Retirement Age (currently age 66).
- At age 70, the higher-earning spouse switches from the Spousal Benefit to his or her maximized Work History Benefit.

If the higher-earning spouse reaches his or her Full Retirement Age and has not claimed any benefit, but the lower-earning spouse has already claimed his or her own Work History Benefit, then the higher-earning spouse can choose between claiming a Spousal Benefit or their own Work History Benefit. If he or she chooses to restrict their benefit to only a Spousal Benefit at Full Retirement Age, the still-unclaimed Work History Benefit will earn Delayed Retirement Credits and grow by 8% per year, until age 70. At any time between Full Retirement Age and age 70, he or she can switch from the Spousal Benefit to his or her higher Work History Benefit.

With the higher-earning spouse waiting until Full Retirement Age of 66 to claim a Spousal Benefit, he or she will be able to accomplish two vitally important objectives:

> **1. He or she will receive the highest Spousal Benefit of 50% of the other spouse's Work History Benefit at his or her Full Retirement Age.**

> **2. He or she gains the option to later switch from the Spousal Benefit to their own much higher Work History Benefit.**

Between age 66 and age 69, while the higher-earning spouse is receiving a Spousal Benefit, he or she continues to earn Delayed Retirement Credits on the unclaimed Work History Benefit of 8% annually. It is crucial to understand that by claiming his or her Work History Benefit at age 70, the higher-earner also benefits from what I call the Social Security Time Machine. He or she will retroactively receive COLA increases from the previous eight years. This adjustment should increase the Work History Benefit significantly.

WHEN THE HIGHER-EARNING SPOUSE CLAIMS A SPOUSAL BENEFIT AT THEIR FULL RETIREMENT AGE, HE OR SHE MUST INFORM THE SOCIAL SECURITY ADMINISTRATION OF THE DECISION TO RESTRICT HIS OR HER BENEFIT TO ONLY A SPOUSAL BENEFIT.

It frequently makes sense for the lower-earning spouse to claim as early as possible. This provides the married couple with a decent amount of Social

Security income and makes it easier for the higher-earner to maximize his or her benefit.

CASE STUDY: CRIS AND LEE WEIGH THE OPTIONS

Cris and Lee are considering both the Claim As Early As Possible strategy and the Claim Early, Claim Late strategy. They decide to run the numbers for both options so they can evaluate which approach is better for their particular circumstances. Table 12.1 illustrates their analysis for the Claim As Early As Possible strategy. Table 12.2 shows the Claim Early, Claim Late—Getting Paid To Wait strategy. As with the other Cris and Lee case studies, I have assumed both spouses are the same age. I have assumed Cris was age 62 before January 1, 2016 and is the higher-earning spouse with a Full Retirement Age Work History Benefit of $1,500 per month. I have assumed Lee is the lower-earning spouse with a Work History Benefit, at her Full Retirement Age (age 66), of $1,125 per month.

TABLE 12.1

CLAIM AS EARLY AS POSSIBLE

CLAIM AS EARLY AS POSSIBLE
Lee's Full Retirement Age Benefit - $1,125. Cris's Full Retirement Age Benefit - $1,500.

A	B	C	D	E	F
Age	Lee's Monthly Income	Cris's Monthly Income	Combined Monthly Income	Combined Annual Income	Cumulative Annual Income
62	$845	$1,125	$1,970	$23,640	$23,640
63	$870	$1,158	$2,028	$24,336	$47,976
64	$896	$1,193	$2,089	$25,068	$73,044
65	$923	$1,229	$2,152	$25,824	$98,868
66	$951	$1,266	$2,217	$26,604	$125,472
67	$979	$1,304	$2,283	$27,396	$152,868
68	$1,008	$1,343	$2,351	$28,212	$181,080
69	$1,039	$1,383	$2,422	$29,064	$210,144
70	$1,070	$1,425	$2,495	$29,940	$240,084

Assumed an annual COLA increase of 3.00%

THE CLAIM AS EARLY AS POSSIBLE STRATEGY

In Table 12.1, Cris and Lee use the Claim As Early As Possible strategy and both claim their Social Security Work History Benefits at age 62, as seen in Column A. When a number in Column A has a rectangle around it, this means either both spouses or one of the spouses claimed their benefit at that age. Because they claimed their benefits early at age 62, both of their monthly checks were reduced by 25% to $845 per month for Lee in Column B (the exact amount is actually $843.75, but I rounded it up to $845) and $1,125 per month for Cris in Column C. Both of those numbers also have rectangles around them signifying that they are newly claimed benefits. Add their monthly income checks together and the total is $1,970 ($845 + $1,125), which appears in Column D. Their Combined Annual Income of $23,640 is shown in Column E. This is the amount of Social Security income they are going to receive every year for the rest of their lives. Their income will increase a small amount each year because of the assumed annual COLA increase of 3%. The last column, the Cumulative Annual Income, or Column F, keeps a running total of all the Social Security income Cris and Lee have earned up to that particular year. Later on, I will use the numbers in Column F to show you how much money Cris and Lee were Paid to Wait.

TABLE 12.2

CLAIM EARLY, CLAIM LATE

Lee's Full Retirement Age Benefit - $1,125. Cris's Full Retirement Age Benefit - $1,500.

A	B	C	D	E	F
Age	Lee's Monthly Income	Cris's Monthly Income	Combined Monthly Income	Combined Annual Income	Cumulative Annual Income
62	$845	$0	$845	$10,140	$10,140
63	$870	$0	$870	$10,440	$20,580
64	$896	$0	$896	$10,752	$31,332
65	$923	$0	$923	$11,076	$42,408
66	$951	$633	$1,584	$19,008	$61,416
67	$979	$651	$1,630	$19,560	$80,976
68	$1,008	$671	$1,679	$20,148	$101,124
69	$1,039	$691	$1,730	$20,760	$121,884
70	$1,070	$2,508	$3,578	$42,936	$164,820

Assumed an annual COLA increase of 3.00%

$121,884 was the amount of money this married couple was 'Paid to Wait'.

CLAIM EARLY, CLAIM LATE— THE GETTING PAID TO WAIT STRATEGY

In Table 12.2, Cris and Lee analyze the Claim Early, Claim Late strategy. In this case, it was assumed that Cris was age 62 or older before January 1, 2016. With this strategy, there is also a rectangle around the number 62 in the age column, or Column A, but in this case only Lee claims her benefit at age 62 of $845. Cris doesn't claim any benefit at age 62, so there is a $0 in Column C for Cris's monthly income. From age 62 to age 65, Cris and Lee receive only Lee's benefit, which starts out at $845 per month and $10,140 for the year. Age 66 is the next number in Column A with a rectangle around it. That is because at age 66, Cris claims and restricts his benefit to only a Spousal Benefit and starts to receive a Social Security check of $633 per month. The number $633 appears in a rectangle because it is a newly claimed benefit. At age 66, Cris and Lee's Combined Monthly Income (Column D) increases to $1,584 and their Combined Annual Income (Column E) increases to $19,008.

Even though Cris is receiving some Social Security income in the form of a Spousal Benefit, he continues to delay claiming his own Work History Benefit and receives Delayed Retirement Credits. These Delayed Retirement Credits will increase the amount of his unclaimed Work History Benefit by 8% for every year that he delays. You can see the effects of earning Delayed Retirement Credits at age 70, the last number in Column A within a rectangle. At age 70, Cris switches from the Spousal Benefit to his maxed-out (the largest check he can receive from Social Security) Work History Benefit of $2,508 per month (Column C). His monthly check of $2,508 includes four years of Delayed Retirement Credits plus eight years of Retroactive COLA Credits. On the Age 70 line, Cris and Lee's Combined Monthly Income (Column D) increases substantially to $3,578 and their Combined Annual Income (Column E) jumps up to $42,936. Their Cumulative Annual Income, at age 69, is $121,884.

Before we compare the numbers for the two strategies, I want to point out a couple of things. In Table 12.2, Cris and Lee are claiming Social Security benefits at three different ages. They claim benefits at ages 62, 66, and 70. Lee claims her Work History Benefit at age 62 and Cris claims a Spousal Benefit at age 66. Then, Cris claims his Work History Benefit at age 70. When Cris claims his maxed-out Work History Benefit at age 70, he stops receiving the Spousal Benefit. With the Claim As Early As Possible strategy in Table 12.1, Cris and Lee only claim two benefits, their Work History Benefits at age 62. With the Claim Early, Claim Late strategy in Table 12.2, they claim three Social Security benefits, including Cris's maxed-out Work History Benefit at age 70.

COMPARING THE TWO STRATEGIES
COMBINED ANNUAL INCOME AT AGE 66

TABLE 12.3

	A	B	C	D	E	F
	Age	Lee's Monthly Income	Cris's Monthly Income	Combined Monthly Income	*Combined Annual Income	Cumulative Annual Income
Claim as Early as Possible	66	$951	$1,266	$2,217	$26,604	S125,472
Claim Early, Claim Late	66	$951	$633	$1,584	$19,008	$61,416

* Starting at age 66, the Claim Early, Claim Late strategy pays the married couple 71% of the income they would have received with the Claim as Early as Possible Strategy ($19,008 ÷ $26,604 = 71%).

Let's compare the results of the two strategies by examining the numbers that are circled in both tables. Table 12.3 compares the Social Security income numbers for each strategy at age 66. The Claim As Early As Possible numbers are on the top line and the Claim Early, Claim Late numbers are on the bottom line. Column E, Combined Annual Income, shows that, at age 66, the Claim Early, Claim Late strategy pays the couple $19,008 for that year, while the Claim As Early As Possible strategy pays them $26,604. Therefore, at age 66, the Claim Early, Claim Late strategy would pay the couple 71% of the income they would earn if they choose the Claim As Early As Possible strategy ($19,008/$26,604 = 71%). Keep in mind that the entire time the Claim Early, Claim Late strategy is paying Cris and Lee an income of $19, 008, Cris is still delaying the claiming of his own Work History Benefit and it is growing by 8% per year.

CUMULATIVE ANNUAL INCOME AT AGE 69—
THE AMOUNT OF MONEY THEY WERE PAID TO WAIT

TABLE 12.4

	A	B	C	D	E	F
	Age	Lee's Monthly Income	Cris's Monthly Income	Combined Monthly Income	Combined Annual Income	Cumulative Annual Income
Claim as Early as Possible	69	$1,039	$1,383	$2,422	$29,064	$210,144
Claim Early, Claim Late	69	$1,039	$691	$1,730	$20,760	*$121,884

* While Cris was delaying claiming his Work History Benefit until age 70, the couple still received $121,884 of Social Security income. In other words, they were "paid" $121,884 to "wait".

Table 12.4 compares the Claim As Early As Possible (numbers are on the top line) and the Claim Early, Claim Late (numbers are on the bottom line) at age 69. Column F, Cumulative Annual Income, represents the total amount of Social Security income Cris and Lee will earn over the eight-year period from ages 62 through 69. The Claim As Early As Possible Cumulative Annual Income figure of $210,144 is larger than the Claim Early, Claim Late total of $121,884. However, keep in mind that the couple received this $121,884 while Cris still has not claimed his maxed-out Work History Benefit. Thus, the entire time Cris waited to claim his maxed-out Work History Benefit at age 70, the couple still received $121,884 of Social Security income. This is how they were getting paid to wait. In this case, they are paid $121,844 to wait.

CUMULATIVE ANNUAL INCOME AT AGE 70—
THE TIPPING POINT

Up until this point, Cris and Lee would have received more total Social Security income if they had used the Claim As Early As Possible strategy, but things are about to change dramatically. At age 70, Cris and Lee's Social Security income with the Claim Early, Claim Late strategy is so much larger than the income they receive from the Claim As Early As Possible strategy, it will take them a relatively short period of time to make up the difference. At age 70, Cris and Lee are in much better shape financially by using the Claim Early, Claim Late strategy.

COMPARING THE RESULTS

TABLE 12.5

	A	B	C	D	E	F
	Age	Lee's Monthly Income	Cris's Monthly Income	Combined Monthly Income	Combined Annual Income	Cumulative Annual Income
Claim as Early as Possible	70	$1,070	$1,425	$2,495	$29,940	$240,084
Claim Early, Claim Late	70	$1,070	$2,508	$3,578	$42,936	$164,820

Table 12.5 compares the numbers at age 70. In Column C, you see that Cris's Monthly Income with the Claim As Early As Possible strategy is only $1,425. With the Claim Early, Claim Late strategy, Cris' Monthly Income at age 70 is substantially higher at $2,508. Cris was able to maximize the size of his Work History Benefit and received a monthly Social Security check that was $1,083 larger ($2,508 - $1,425 = $1,083) than the size of the check he would have received if he chose the Claim As Early As Possible strategy. The size of Cris' Monthly Income at age 70 also represents the amount of the Survivor Benefit. After the first spouse dies, the surviving spouse is going to receive only one check. He or she will receive the larger of the two checks. If Cris and Lee choose the Claim Early, Claim Late strategy, the surviving spouse will receive a much larger Survivor Benefit of $2,508.

Now look at Column D, the Combined Monthly Income column: $2,495 for the Claim As Early As Possible strategy and $3,578 for the Claim Early,

Claim Late strategy. Beginning at age 70, Cris and Lee's Combined Monthly Income from both Social Security checks is much higher using the Claim Early, Claim Late strategy.

Column E, the Combined Annual Income column, shows the total amount of Social Security income the couple will receive for that year. With the Claim As Early As Possible strategy, they will receive $29,940. With the Claim Early, Claim Late strategy, they will receive $42,936 for the year. That's a difference of $12,996 more Social Security income with the Claim Early, Claim Late strategy. Also remember, because of COLA, their Social Security income should increase every year, but, because the benefits at age 70 are so much larger with the Claim Early, Claim Late strategy, they will receive larger dollar increases with that strategy, and the initial difference of $12,996 is only going to get larger over time.

At age 70, life will be so much better for Cris and Lee if they choose the Claim Early, Claim Late strategy. They will enjoy more income and also a much larger Survivor Benefit. The results for the Claim Early, Claim Late strategy get more incredible after age 70, but it is all about getting to age 70. The Claim Early, Claim Late strategy can make it much easier to do that because while Cris was delaying his benefit, they were paid $121,844 while they waited.

TWO CHECKS IN ONE

The Claim Early, Claim Late strategy often results in one Survivor Benefit check being larger than the combined total of the two Social Security checks the couple would receive if they used the Claim As Early As Possible strategy (both spouses claiming their benefits at age 62).

TABLE 12.6

	A	B	C	D	E	F
	Age	Lee's Monthly Income	Cris's Monthly Income	Combined Monthly Income	Combined Annual Income	Cumulative Annual Income
Claim as Early as Possible	70	$1,070	$1,425	$2,495	$29,940	$240,084
Claim Early, Claim Late	70	$1,070	$2,508	$3,578	$42,936	$164,820

Cris's ONE check is bigger than the combined total of TWO checks.

The numbers in Table 12.6 are the same numbers that appear in Table 12.5. Table 12.6 compares the Combined Monthly Income of $2,495 for the Claim As Early As Possible strategy with Cris's Monthly Income of $2,508 for the Claim Early, Claim Late strategy. The $2,495 circled in Column D for their Combined Monthly Income column represents the combined total of the TWO Social Security checks that Cris and Lee will receive when they are both alive. The number $2,508 circled in the Cris's Monthly Income column indicates the amount of the ONE check that Cris will receive, which will eventually become the Survivor Benefit check. The amount of Cris's ONE check of $2,508 with the Claim Early, Claim Late strategy is larger than the combined total of $2,495 the couple will receive from the TWO checks while they are both alive, if they choose the Claim As Early As Possible strategy.

Observe that, in Column F, Cumulative Annual Income, the total for the Claim As Early As Possible strategy, $240,084, is larger than the Cumulative Annual Income amount of $164,820 for the Claim Early, Claim Late strategy. Because Cris and Lee's combined Social Security income at age 70 and beyond is so much larger under the Claim Early, Claim Late strategy, they will be able to close the income gap in a relatively short period of time—after age 70.

CLOSING THE GAP AFTER AGE 70

I am going to show you what happens after age 70 and how the Claim Early, Claim Late strategy quickly makes up for the lower amount of money Cris and Lee receive between age 62 and age 69. I am also going to show you how the Claim Early, Claim Late strategy eventually pays them hundreds of thousands of dollars in additional Social Security income if just one of the spouses lives until their life expectancy. However, before I do that, I need to make you aware of a critically important point:

IT'S ALL ABOUT GETTING TO AGE 70.

If you are a married couple and decide to use the Claim Early, Claim Late strategy then, at age 70, you and your spouse are in one of the best possible positions to take full advantage of your Social Security benefits and all they have to offer. It really doesn't matter what happens after age 70, because you have better optimized your Social Security benefits and positioned yourselves for a more financially secure retirement.

IT REALLY IS ALL ABOUT GETTING TO AGE 70

Every married couple should consider three things before making their Social Security claiming decision:

• Longevity

• COLA

• The Survivor Benefit

1.) Longevity and Guaranteed Lifetime Income

When we examined the Why Wait Factor #1 (You're Probably Going to Live Longer Than You Think), we discussed the fact that the biggest risk people face in their retirement is the risk of living too long and running out of money too soon. We identified longevity as not only one of the primary threats to retirement income, but as the threat magnifier. One of the best ways to reduce the longevity threat is to get a higher amount of guaranteed lifetime income. If you receive a higher amount of guaranteed lifetime income, it should make it easier for you to pay your bills and maintain your financial independence, no matter how long you live. Because guaranteed lifetime income reduces the financial risk of living too long, it is a form of longevity insurance. Social Security pays you guaranteed lifetime income; it is also a form of longevity insurance.

By using the Claim Early, Claim Late strategy, you can substantially increase your Social Security income starting at age 70, providing you with a much larger amount of guaranteed lifetime income, which greatly reduces your financial risk of living too long. If living too long is the greatest financial risk you face in your retirement, the Claim Early, Claim Late strategy significantly reduces that risk and offers you and your spouse far greater security during your retirement.

2.) Compounding the COLA Benefit

When we examined the Why Wait Factor #4 (The Pay Increase Benefit), I showed you how to maximize the COLA benefit by applying the COLA percentage increase to the highest possible number. This is what happens at age 70 if you use the Claim Early, Claim Late strategy. Cris and Lee's combined Social Security income is much larger at age 70 using the Claim Early, Claim Late strategy, which means they will receive larger pay raises every year for the rest of their lives.

At age 70, it really doesn't matter how high the inflation rate is; whether it is small or large, the COLA increase is going to be applied to a much larger number, ensuring that Cris and Lee receive much larger pay raises every year for the rest of their lives. From a Social Security perspective, by choosing the Claim Early, Claim Late strategy, at age 70, you are in one of the best possible positions to keep up with inflation because you took full advantage of the compounding effect of the COLA feature.

3.) Maximizing the Survivor Benefit

The Claim Early, Claim Late strategy also maximizes the size of the Survivor Benefit at age 70. Speaking in purely financial terms, beginning at age 70, it doesn't matter when the first spouse dies. When that happens, the surviving spouse is left with the largest Survivor Benefit check possible. If either you or your spouse dies a short time after age 70, it should be comforting to know that the surviving spouse will receive the largest Survivor Benefit check possible. Even if the first spouse dies many years after age 70, the surviving spouse is still left with the largest Survivor Benefit possible.

Very early in the book I pointed out that it's usually the wife who suffers the consequences if the husband claims his Social Security at age 62, and she is left with the smallest Survivor Benefit possible, which increases the chances that she will struggle financially after he dies. By using the Claim Early, Claim Late strategy, the husband makes a much better decision, and his wife enjoys the benefits of this decision with a much larger amount of Social Security income while they are both alive and the largest Survivor Benefit possible.

FOR THOSE WHO ALSO HAVE ACCUMULATED SAVINGS

Don't make the mistake of thinking that the Claim Early, Claim Late strategy is not relevant if you are fortunate enough to have some accumulated savings, or even a substantial amount of accumulated savings. Everyone hopes their savings will last as long as they are alive. Choosing the Claim Early, Claim Late strategy will provide you with a much larger amount of Social Security income, which should decrease the amount of money you have to withdraw from you accumulated savings in order to pay your bills. Decreasing the amount of money you have to withdraw from your savings should greatly increase the probability that your savings will last as long as you do.

IF ONE OF YOUR BIGGEST CONCERNS IS MAKING SURE YOU DON'T RUN OUT OF MONEY BEFORE YOU RUN OUT OF BREATH, THEN CHOOSING THE CLAIM EARLY, CLAIM LATE STRATEGY COULD BE ONE OF THE BEST THINGS YOU COULD DO TO DECREASE THE CHANCES OF THAT HAPPENING.

WHAT HAPPENS AFTER AGE 70? THE BIG PAY DAY

Let's look at what happens to the numbers after age 70. How many years does it take Cris and Lee to break even if they use the Claim Early, Claim Late strategy instead of the Claim As Early As Possible strategy? Let's also look at the amount of Social Security income the couple would receive with each strategy if they lived to age 80 or age 85.

TABLE 12.7

	A	B	C	D	E	F	G
	Age	Lee's Monthly Income	Cris's Monthly Income	Combined Monthly Income	Combined Annual Income	Cumulative Annual Income	Difference
Claim as Early as Possible	76	$1,278	$1,701	$2,979	$37,748	($439,512)	
Claim Early, Claim Late	76	$1,278	$2,994	$4,272	$51,264	($450,828)	$11,316

Table 12.7 shows how long it will take the married couple to break even if they use the Claim Early, Claim Late strategy. I added one additional column to the table, Column G, or the Difference column. This column shows the difference in the total amount of Social Security income the married couple would have earned with the Claim Early, Claim Late strategy. In Table 12.7, you see that the couple breaks even at age 76 (Column A). Both numbers for each strategy are circled in Column F. By age 76, the married couple would have earned a cumulative, total amount of Social Security income of $439,512 with the Claim As Early As Possible strategy and $450,828 if they had used the Claim Early, Claim Late strategy. In fact, they would have earned $11,316 (Column G) more with the Claim Early, Claim Late strategy. Therefore, by age 76, the married couple would have broken even and made up for the lower amount of Social Security income that they would have earned between ages 62-69.

TABLE 12.8

	A	B	C	D	E	F	G
	Age	Lee's Monthly Income	Cris's Monthly Income	Combined Monthly Income	Combined Annual Income	Cumulative Annual Income	Difference
Claim as Early as Possible	80	$1,438	($1,915)	$3,353	($40,236)	($593,544)	
Claim Early, Claim Late	80	$1,438	($3,370)	$4,808	($57,696)	($671,724)	($78,180)

Table 12.8 shows the differences between the two strategies at age 80 (Column A). More numbers are circled in this table to illustrate how the dollar difference between the two strategies grows larger over time. The numbers grow bigger over time because I assumed an annual COLA increase of 3%. You can see that bigger dollar difference between the two strategies with the numbers circled in Column C for Cris's Monthly Income and Column E for their Combined Annual Income. The numbers in Column F are also circled and show Cumulative Income of $593,544 with the Claim As Early As Possible strategy and $671,724 with the Claim Early, Claim Late strategy. The number $78,180 is circled in Column G, which represents the amount of additional money the married couple would have earned if they had used the Claim Early, Claim Late strategy.

TABLE 12.9

	A	B	C	D	E	F	G
	Age	Lee's Monthly Income	Cris's Monthly Income	Combined Monthly Income	Combined Annual Income	Cumulative Annual Income	Difference
Claim as Early as Possible	85	$1,667	$2,220	$3,887	$46,644	($813,552)	
Claim Early, Claim Late	85	$1,667	$3,907	$5,574	$66,888	($987,240)	$173,688

Table 12.9 shows the differences between the two strategies at age 85. In Column G, you see that the difference between the two strategies has grown to $173,688. At age 85, Cris and Lee would have earned $173,688 more by using the Claim Early, Claim Late strategy. If the couple lives past age 85, the income difference between the two strategies would grow even larger. If they live until age 90, the difference would approach $300,000.

WHAT HAPPENS IF ONE SPOUSE DIES BEFORE THEY BREAK EVEN?

You may be concerned about what would happen if one of the spouses dies in their early or mid-70s. Will the numbers for the Claim Early, Claim Late strategy not be as impressive? Would the couple have been better off using the Claim As Early As Possible strategy? Let's examine this concern.

If one of the spouses passes away in his or her early 70s, the numbers do not change significantly. The break even age would stay more or less the same at age 76. If one of the spouses passes away in their early 70s, it may push the break even age out to age 77; otherwise, it stays at age 76. After the first spouse dies, the surviving spouse receives only one check instead of two, but the fact remains that the break even age is not meaningfully impacted, if at all.

If Cris and Lee use the Claim Early, Claim Late strategy after the higher-earning spouse claims at age 70, only one spouse must live to age 76 or 77 to break even. If only one of the spouses lives past age 76 or 77, he or she would be much better off using the Claim Early, Claim Late strategy because not only would they be left with a much bigger Survivor Benefit, but he or she would receive more cumulative Social Security income over their retirement lifetime. In fact, if only one spouse lives until age 80, he or she will still receive tens of thousands of dollars in additional Social Security income by using the Claim Early, Claim Late strategy. If one spouse lives until age 85, he or she will still receive well over $100,000 of additional Social Security income.

Referring back to Table 12.7 and 12.8, if Cris and Lee choose the Claim Early, Claim Late strategy, they break even at age 76 and make an additional $78,180 at age 80. Ages 76 and 80 are below the average life expectancies for both of them, and only one of them has to be alive to receive the benefits of using the Claim Early, Claim Late strategy. In Table 12.9, by age 85, the couple will earn an additional $173,688. Age 85 is a little higher than Cris's life expectancy of age 84, but it is still younger than Lee's life expectancy of age 86. Only one of the spouses must be alive at age 85 in order to have earned well over $100,000 of additional Social Security income.

All of the great results that happen after age 70 with the Claim Early, Claim Late strategy don't come about unless the higher-earning spouse delays claiming his or her benefits until age 70. The crucial issue is to make it easy for the spouse with the larger benefit to delay claiming as long as possible, ideally until age 70, and that is exactly what the Claim Early, Claim Late strategy does.

CASE STUDY: PAT AND CORY EXPLORE ANOTHER VARIATION OF CLAIM EARLY, CLAIM LATE

There are many variations of the Claim Early, Claim Late strategy. You are not limited to the Cris and Lee approach we discussed above, although I do believe this approach is appropriate for many married couples. The version of the Claim Early, Claim Late strategy that I used in the Cris and Lee example is the one strategy that will pay them the most amount of money while they wait.

A variation of the Claim Early, Claim Late strategy is illustrated by the case of Pat—the lower-earning spouse—and Cory—the higher-earning spouse who was age 62 or older before January 1, 2016. Their Full Retirement Age benefits are exactly the same as Lee and Cris's Full Retirement Age Benefits from the previous example. Pat's Full Retirement Age Benefit is $1,125 per month and Cory's is $1,500 per month. You can compare the numbers for this version of the Claim Early, Claim Late strategy with the numbers for the previous Claim As Early As Possible strategy. (Table 12.1)

In this example, instead of Pat claiming a Work History Benefit at 62, she claims it at her Full Retirement Age of 66. Pat has decided to continue working until age 66 and will make more than $15,720 in 2016. If a person claims his or her Social Security benefits at age 62, continues to work, and makes more than $15,720 in 2016 on the job, she will have to give back some of her benefits. Pat was thinking about claiming her Social Security benefits at age 62 but realized she would probably end up paying most of the money back because of the amount of her salary, so she decided to delay claiming her benefits until age 66. Once Pat reaches her Full Retirement Age of 66, she can continue to work and make as much money as she wanted and not have to pay back any of her Social Security benefits.

If you will reach your Full Retirement Age after 2016 and continue to work, for every $2 you earn in excess of $15,720, you will have to pay back $1 of your Social Security benefits. If you reach your Full Retirement Age in 2016 and continue to work, for every $3 you earn in excess of $41,880, you will have to pay back $1 of your Social Security benefits. No earnings received after Full Retirement Age are subject to the earnings test.[1] These earnings limits are updated every year and are increased by the same COLA percentage increase that every Social Security recipient receives.

TABLE 12.10

Pat's Full Retirement Age Benefit - $1,125, Cory's Full Retirement Age Benefit - $1,500.

A	B	C	D	E	F
Age	Pat's Monthly Income	Cory's Monthly Income	Combined Monthly Income	Combined Annual Income	Cumulative Annual Income
62	$0	$0	$0	$0	$0
63	$0	$0	$0	$0	$0
64	$0	$0	$0	$0	$0
65	$0	$0	$0	$0	$0
66	$1,266	$633	$1,899	$22,788	$22,788
67	$1,304	$651	$1,955	$23,460	$46,248
68	$1,343	$671	$2,014	$24,168	$70,146
69	$1,383	$691	$2,074	$24,888	$95,304
70	$1,425	$2,508	$3,933	$47,196	$142,500

Assumed an annual COLA increase of 3.00%

$95,304 was the amount of money this married couple was 'Paid to Wait'.

Table 12.10 shows the numbers for this version of the Claim Early, Claim Late strategy. In the Age column, only two numbers appear in a square; ages 66 and 70. At age 66, both Pat and Cory claim a Social Security benefit. Pat claims a Work History Benefit, and receives $1,266 per month (Column B). The $1,266 per month that Pat receives at age 66 is Pat's Full Retirement Age Benefit of $1,125 per month, plus four years of Retroactive COLA Credits. The four years of Retroactive COLA Credits increase the amount that Pat receives from $1,125 to $1,266 per month. Cory claims a Spousal Benefit at age 66 and receives 50% of Pat's benefit, or $633 per month (Column C). At age 66, their Combined Monthly Income (Column D) is $1,899 and their Combined Annual Income (Column E) is $22,788. If we compare Pat and Cory's Combined Annual Income in Table 12.10 of $22,788 with the Combined Annual Income for the Claim As Early As Possible strategy at age 66 in Table 12.1 of $26,604, you will notice that the numbers are fairly close. In fact, this version of the Claim Early, Claim Late strategy will pay the couple 85% ($22,788/$26,604 = 85%) of the income they would have received if they had used the Claim As Early As Possible strategy. As in the earlier case study, Cory, at age 70, switches from a Spousal Benefit to a maximized Work History Benefit of $2,508 and their Combined Annual Income (Column E) increases to $47,196.

You may have noticed that Pat and Cory's Combined Monthly Income (Column D) and Combined Annual Income (Column E), at age 70 (Column A), are even bigger with this version of the Claim Early, Claim Late strategy, but they were paid less money while they waited. You can see that in Column F, the number $95,304 is circled. That is the amount of money Pat and Cory were paid to wait. That number is smaller than the $121,884 from the Cris and Lee version of the Claim Early, Claim Late strategy. (Table 12.2)

AFTER AGE 70

TABLE 12.11

A	B	C	D	E	F	G
Age	Pat's Monthly Income	Cory's Monthly Income	Combined Monthly Income	Combined Annual Income	Cumulative Annual Income	Difference
70	$1,425	$2,508	$3,933	$47,196	$142,492	(-$97,592)
76 (BE)	$1,701	$2,994	$4,695	$56,340	$456,844	$17,102
80	$1,915	$3,370	$5,285	$63,420	$699,652	$105,878
85	$2,220	$3,907	$6,127	$73,524	$1,046,440	$232,658

Table 12.11 demonstrates that the break even age for this strategy has stayed the same at age 76. This happens because even though Pat and Cory received less cumulative Social Security income between ages 62 and 69, Pat's Social Security benefit was larger because it was claimed at age 66. This made their Combined Monthly Income and Combined Annual Income even larger at age 70, which still allowed them to break even at age 76. The numbers at age 80 and 85 are even larger too. Therefore, if you can afford to receive less income while the higher-earning spouse delays claiming until age 70, you may want to use this version of the Claim Early, Claim Late strategy, where the lower-earning spouse claims the Work History Benefit at age 66 because their combined income at age 70, and beyond, will be even larger.

WHAT IF WE ARE NOT THE SAME AGE?

Many married couples are not the same age. Statistically, husbands are an average of three years older than their wives. Does the Claim Early, Claim Late strategy work just as well even if the married couple is not the same age? In most cases, it does; especially if there is not a large difference in age between the husband and wife. In cases where the husband is the higher-earning spouse and the wife is younger than the husband, it's probably more important for the husband to maximize his benefit because his wife will probably live for an even longer period of time after he dies. In this situation, it's even more important for the husband to delay claiming his benefit as long as possible, so he can leave his wife with a bigger Survivor Benefit.

OUR BENEFITS DON'T LOOK ANYTHING LIKE THE ONES IN THE CASE STUDIES!

Your Social Security Benefit numbers may not resemble the numbers used in these case studies. The concept of the Claim Early, Claim Late strategy works very well in many different situations. Remember, it is all about the strategic use of the Spousal Benefit. The amount of Social Security income that the strategy generates will vary depending on your situation. To get a better idea of how the strategy would work in your specific situation, go to my website, www.GettingPaidToWait.com and use the Social Security Calculator, which will tell you if you still qualify to use the Claim Early, Claim Late strategy and then show you how the strategy would work in your specific situation. Using your personal benefit information, the Calculator will tell exactly when and how you and your spouse should claim your Social Security benefits.

CHAPTER 12 IMPORTANT CONCEPTS:

•The Claim Early, Claim Late strategy will pay qualified married couples the most amount of Social Security income while they wait for the spouse with the larger benefit to claim it at age 70.

• The key to the Claim Early, Claim Late strategy is the unconventional way it uses your Secret Weapon, the Spousal Benefit.

• For people who have money saved, choosing the Claim Early, Claim Late strategy can greatly increase the probability that your accumulated savings will last as long as you do.

• By using the Claim Early, Claim Late strategy instead of the Claim as Early as Possible strategy, only one spouse has to live until their life expectancy in order to receive tens of thousands of dollars, or even hundreds of thousands of dollars, of additional Social Security income.

• If you are a qualified married couple, the Claim Early, Claim Late strategy can put you in one of the best possible positions to take better advantage of your Social Security benefits and all they have to offer.

• Using the Claim Early, Claim Late strategy provides a qualified married couple with the biggest Survivor Benefit possible in their situation. Many times, that one Survivor Benefit is like TWO checks in ONE.

• The Claim Early, Claim Late strategy addresses the three things that every married couple should consider before making their Social Security claiming decision: Longevity, COLA , The Survivor Benefit.

• The crucial issue is to make it easy for the spouse with the larger benefit to delay claiming as long as possible, ideally until age 70, and that is exactly what the Claim Early, Claim Late strategy does.

SOURCES

1. Social Security Administration, Exempt Amounts Under The Earnings Test (United States: SSA, 2014)

FILE AND SUSPEND
USE IT OR LOSE IT

THE STRATEGY THAT MAXIMIZES BOTH BENEFITS

If you are age 66 or older before May 1, 2016, you are still eligible to use the File and Suspend strategy explained and illustrated in this chapter. But if you want to use the version of the strategy in which one spouse claims a Spousal Benefit after the other spouse "suspends" their benefit, you must actually implement the strategy before May 1, 2016. So, even if you qualify to use the version of the File and Suspend strategy illustrated in this chapter, if you fail to implement it before May 1, 2016, you will lose the right to use the strategy. In other words: USE IT BEFORE MAY 1, 2016, OR LOSE IT!

To determine if you still qualify to use the File and Suspend strategy, please visit my website at www.gettingpaidtowait.com and use my Paid to Wait Social Security Calculator. The Paid to Wait Social Security Calculator will tell you if you are qualified to use the strategy and then show you exactly how it would work for your personal situation.

The File and Suspend strategy is another way the Social Security Administration gives qualified married couples every opportunity to maximize their benefits. It is also another way you can get paid to wait. However, for many married couples, the File and Suspend strategy will usually pay them less Social Security income than the Claim Early, Claim Late strategy while they are delaying claiming their benefits. However, the File and Suspend strategy can maximize the size of both spouse's Social Security Work History Benefits and pay you and your spouse the most Social Security income at age 70 and beyond.

WHY WOULD YOU FILE AND IMMEDIATELY SUSPEND?

If you are qualified, the Social Security Administration gives you the option of filing for retirement benefits, and then requesting that the payments be suspended. You can literally file for your benefits and immediately suspend them, hence the name of this strategy: File and Suspend. Why would you do that?

A spouse cannot claim a Spousal Benefit until the other spouse has claimed his or her own Work History Benefit. If the higher-earning spouse wants to delay the claiming of his or her Work History Benefit as long as possible, for instance, until age 70, his or her spouse cannot claim a Spousal Benefit until age 70. This fact makes the prospect of delaying claiming until age 70 much less attractive. However, this does not have to be the case! The higher-earning spouse can file for his or her Work History Benefit at age 66 (assumed Full Retirement Age) and immediately suspend the payments.

HOW THIS STRATEGY WORKS:

1. Because the higher-earning spouse technically claimed his or her Work History Benefit at Full Retirement Age, the spouse with the lower Work History Benefit can now claim his or her Spousal Benefit. If he or she is Full Retirement Age when claiming the Spousal Benefit, they are entitled to receive 50% of the higher-earning spouse's Work History Benefit.

2. Because the higher-earning spouse filed for his or her Work History Benefit and immediately suspended the receipt of any payments (which means he or she does not receive any monthly Social Security checks), he or she will continue to earn Delayed Retirement Credits on his or her own Social Security Work History Benefit. This means, for every year after Full Retirement Age, which is currently age 66, the amount of his or her Work History Benefit will increase by 8% annually. Therefore, by waiting until

age 70 to un-suspend his or her Work History Benefit, the size of the benefit will be maximized. This will allow the higher-earning spouse to receive the largest Social Security check possible for the rest of his or her life, and if he or she passes away first, for the rest of their spouse's life as well.

THERE IS ONE VERY IMPORTANT CONDITION THAT NEEDS TO BE SATISFIED IN ORDER TO USE THE FILE AND SUSPEND STRATEGY—THE HIGHER-EARNING SPOUSE WHO FILES AND SUSPENDS MUST BE AT FULL RETIREMENT AGE OR OLDER.

FILE AND SUSPEND WITH CRIS AND LEE

TABLE 13.1

Lee's Full Retirement Age Benefit - $500, Cris's full Retirement Age Benefit - $1,500.

A	B	C	D	E	F
Age	Lee's Monthly Income	Cris's Monthly Income	Combined Monthly Income	Combined Annual Income	Cumulative Annual Income
62	$0	$0	$0	$0	$0
63	$0	$0	$0	$0	$0
64	$0	$0	$0	$0	$0
65	$0	$0	$0	$0	$0
66	$844	$0 (F&S)	$844	$10,128	$10,128
67	$869	$0	$869	$10,428	$20,556
68	$895	$0	$895	$10,740	$31,296
69	$922	$0	$922	$11,064	$42,360
70	$950	$2,508	$3,458	$41,496	$83,856

Assumed an annual COLA increase of 3.00%

$42,360 was the amount of money this married couple was Paid to Wait.

Table 13.1 assumes that Cris and Lee are the same age and Cris was age 66 or older before May 1, 2016. Lee's Full Retirement Age Work History

Benefit is $500 per month and Cris's is $1,500 per month.

At age 66, Cris files for his Work History Benefit and immediately suspends it. You can see that in Column C for Cris's Monthly Income, there is a $0 (F&S) on that line. The F&S stands for File and Suspend. Cris does not receive a monthly Social Security check and his suspended Work History Benefit earns Delayed Retirement Credits and grows by 8% per year. By Cris filing and suspending at age 66, Lee is able to claim a Spousal Benefit of $844 at age 66. Lee's Spousal Benefit of $844 is much bigger than her regular Work History Benefit of only $500. Beginning at age 66 and continuing through age 69, the couple receives only Lee's Spousal Benefit check. The reason Lee was able to receive this additional income from the Spousal Benefit was because Cris was able to File and Suspend his benefit at age 66. Their total cumulative Social Security income at age 69 is $42,360, which is circled in Column F. This is the amount of Social Security income the couple was paid while they waited for Cris to claim his benefit at age 70. At age 70, Cris un-suspends his benefit and starts to receive his maxed out Work History Benefit of $2,508 per month. Their Combined Monthly Income (Column D) increases to $3,458 and their Combined Annual Income (Column E) jumps up to $41,496.

THE BEST OF BOTH WORLDS

Qualified married couples can use a combination of the File and Suspend and Claim Early, Claim Late (Restricted Application) strategies.

TABLE 13.2

Lee's Full Retirement Age Benefit - $1,125, Cris's Full Retirement Age Benefit - $1,500.					
A	B	C	D	E	F
Age	Lee's Monthly Income	Cris's Monthly Income	Combined Monthly Income	Combined Annual Income	Cumulative Annual Income
62	$0	$0	$0	$0	$0
63	$0	$0	$0	$0	$0
64	$0	$0	$0	$0	$0
65	$0	$0	$0	$0	$0
66	$844	$0 (F&S)	$844	$10,128	$10,128
67	$869	$0	$869	$10,428	$20,556
68	$895	$0	$895	$10,740	$31,296
69	$922	$0	$922	$11,064	$42,360
70	$1,881	$2,508	$4,389	$52,668	$95,028

Assumed an annual COLA increase of 3.00%

$42,360 was the amount of money this married couple was 'Paid to Wait'.

Table 13.2 is very similar to Table 13.1 with one important difference that takes place at age 70. Table 13.2 assumes that Cris and Lee are the same age and they are both age 66 before May 1, 2016 with Lee's Full Retirement Age Work History Benefit at $1,125 per month and Cris's at $1,500 per month.

At age 66, Cris files for his Work History Benefit and immediately suspends it. You can see that, at age 66 in Column C for Cris's Monthly Income, there is a $0 (F&S) on that line. The F&S stands for "File and Suspend". By suspending payments, Cris does not receive a monthly Social Security check and his Work History Benefit earns Delayed Retirement Credits and grows by 8% per year. By Cris filing and suspending at age 66, Lee is able to claim and restrict her benefit to only a Spousal Benefit. Lee will then receive a monthly Social Security check of $844 (Column B), which includes four years of Retroactive COLA Credits. By Lee restricting her benefit to only a Spousal Benefit, her regular Work History Benefit also earns Delayed Retirement Credits and grows by 8% per year. It is important to remember that

Lee must wait until her Full Retirement Age (age 66) to claim and restrict her benefit to only a Spousal Benefit in order to have the ability to switch to her own maximized Work History Benefit, later on. Beginning at age 66 and continuing through age 69, the couple receives only Lee's monthly Spousal Benefit check. Their total cumulative Social Security income at age 69 is $42,360, which is circled in Column F. This is the amount of additional Social Security income the couple received by using the combination claiming strategy (File and Suspend & Claim Early, Claim Late). This is also the amount of money the couple was paid while they waited to maximize the amount of both their benefits. Up to this point, the numbers in Table 13.1 and Table 13.2 are identical but at age 70 a number of great things happen in Table 13.2.

CHANGES AT AGE 70:

• Cris un-suspends benefits and begins receiving a maxed-out Work History Benefit of $2,508 per month.

• Lee switches from the Spousal Benefit to a maxed-out Work History Benefit of $1,881 per month.

• Their combined monthly income increases to $4,389, which results in Combined Annual Income of $52,668.

File and Suspend is a very good strategy because, in most cases, both Social Security Benefits are maximized and the combined Social Security income for the couple at age 70 and beyond is the highest it can be. Both strategies: Claim Early, Claim Late and File and Suspend, maximize the size of the Survivor Benefit, so the total amount of Social Security income paid to the surviving spouse will be the same with either strategy. Please remember if you are qualified to use this version of the File and Suspend strategy you must act now and implement the strategy before May 1, 2016, because after that date it is GONE FOREVER!

CHANGES CAN BE MADE

• The spouse who Files and Suspends can un-suspend and start receiving his or her benefits at any time between Full Retirement Age and age 70.
• The other spouse can also switch from his or her Spousal Benefit

to his or her own Work History Benefit at any time between Full Retirement Age and age 70.

DON'T LEAVE IT TO CHANCE

Each claiming situation is unique with varying ages, incomes, and numerous other details. Please visit my website, www.GettingPaidToWait.com, and use my Social Security Calculator. By entering a few pieces of information, it will tell you if you still qualify to use either the File and Suspend, the Claim Early, Claim Late (Restricted Application) or the Combination strategy and will show you which strategy will pay you and your spouse the most amount of Social Security income while you delay the claiming of the larger benefit. It will generate specific information for your particular circumstances, including at what ages you and your spouse should claim your benefits.

EVEN IF YOU HAVE ALREADY CLAIMED BENEFITS, YOU CAN STILL SUSPEND THEM

Everything about the File and Suspend strategy explained and illustrated up until now will no longer be available after April 30, 2016. What I am about to show you will still be available for anybody to use after April 30, 2016. Basically, anybody can still suspend their benefits at their Full Retirement Age. If you suspend your benefits at your Full Retirement Age, you won't receive any Social Security income but your benefit will grow by 8% per year up until age 70. The major change is that no other person can receive a Social Security benefit, such as a Spousal Benefit, based upon your suspended benefit. But there still may be a very good reason to suspend your benefits, especially if you claimed your benefits early.

If you have already claimed your Social Security benefits and are younger than age 70, you can still suspend your benefits and earn Delayed Retirement Credits. You still have to wait until your Full Retirement Age before you can suspend your benefits.

If someone claims their benefits at age 62 and after a couple of years of receiving monthly Social Security checks, they read this book and regret their decision, they still have the option of suspending their benefits at their Full Retirement Age of 66. Once they suspend their benefits, they will stop receiving a monthly

Social Security check, but for every year that their benefits are suspended, they will earn Delayed Retirement Credits and their benefit will grow by 8% per year.

LINDY CHANGES HER MIND

TABLE 13.3

$1,500 - Full Retirement Age Benefit								
AGE	62	63	64	65	66	67	68	69	70
Monthly Benefit	$1,125	$1,158	$1,193	$1,229	Suspend $0	$0	$0	$0	$1,881

Table 13.3 shows how this would work. Lindy has a Full Retirement Age Benefit of $1,500 per month, but because she claimed her benefit at age 62, it is reduced to only $1,125. With an assumed annual COLA increase of 3%, Lindy's monthly Social Security check gets a little bigger every year and grows to $1,229 when she is age 65. She regrets her decision of claiming at age 62 and decides to suspend her benefits at her Full Retirement Age of 66. Once she suspends her benefits at age 66, she will stop receiving monthly Social Security checks. This is illustrated in Table 13.3, where you see $0s for her monthly Social Security income at ages 66–69. During those four years between ages 66 and 69, Lindy's suspended benefit will earn Delayed Retirement Credits and grow by 8% per year. At age 70, she can un-suspend her benefit and receive a monthly Social Security check of $1,881, which includes four years of Delayed Retirement Credits and four years of Retroactive COLA Credits. Lindy will receive this larger benefit for the rest of her life.

It is important to note that if Lindy suspended her benefits after April 30, 2016 and had a spouse who was receiving a Spousal Benefit, her spouse would stop receiving that monthly Spousal Benefit check until Lindy un-suspended her benefits at age 70. Lindy's suspended benefit receives Delayed Retirement Credits and grows by 8% per year up to age 70 but the Spousal Benefit does not.

Both married spouses and single individuals can do this. Even if you claimed your benefits at your Full Retirement Age or later, if you are younger than age 70, you can still suspend your benefits and earn Delayed Retirement Credits.

CHAPTER 13 IMPORTANT CONCEPTS:

• The File and Suspend strategy is another way the Social Security Administration gives qualified married couples every opportunity to maximize their benefits.

• A spouse cannot claim a Spousal Benefit until the other spouse has filed for his or her own Work History Benefit.

• A qualified spouse can file for his or her Work History Benefit at his or her Full Retirement Age and immediately suspend payments, which allows him or her to earn Delayed Retirement Credits and the other spouse to claim a Spousal Benefit.

• The File and Suspend strategy can maximize the size of both spouses' benefits and end up paying the couple the most Social Security income at age 70 and beyond.

• Even if you claimed your benefits early, you can still suspend payments at your Full Retirement Age and earn Delayed Retirement Credits on your suspended benefit of 8% per year, up until age 70.

DIVORCED?
SPECIAL STRATEGIES YOU
NEED TO KNOW ABOUT

The Bipartisan Budget Act of 2015 changed some of the claiming rules for divorced individuals. Just like married spouses, divorced spouses must be age 62 or older before January 1, 2016 to be eligible to use the Restricted Application claiming strategy.

Social Security offers a multitude of options for divorced spouses who were married for at least 10 years to increase their Social Security income. It is critical for divorced men and women to take advantage of these options, so they can receive a higher amount of Social Security income and decrease the chances that either spouse will struggle financially in their retirement.

BILL AND JILL GET DIVORCED

Referring back to the Bill and Jill story from Chapter 8, if they were to divorce sometime in their 50s, their financial situation would be very different from the story we previously told. Bill would be in sufficient financial shape because he would receive a large Social Security benefit when he retires. Jill, on the other hand, would not be in a good position because she has a much smaller Work History Benefit and, in turn, a smaller Social Security check. Jill's smaller check would not be a problem if they had stayed married because they would receive two Social Security checks, the combined total of which would allow them to live fairly comfortably during their retirement.

THE AGE GROUP IN THIS COUNTRY EXPERIENCING THE LARGEST RATE OF GROWTH IN THE NUMBER OF DIVORCES OVER THE LAST TWENTY YEARS ARE PEOPLE OVER THE AGE OF 50.[1]

If they divorced in their 50s, Jill would likely be forced to survive on her smaller Social Security check. Divorcing sometime in her 50s does not give Jill a lot of time to make up for the years when she made little money, or for the years when she did not work at all and chose to spend time caring for their children at home. This is why a divorce after age 50 can be financially devastating to the wife. That is also why approximately 20% of divorced, single women, over the age of 65, live in poverty. The percentage is even higher if you include the number of divorced women who live in near poverty.

DIVORCED WOMEN HAVE ONE OF THE HIGHEST RISKS OF LIVING IN POVERTY OR STRUGGLING FINANCIALLY DURING RETIREMENT.[2]

THE SILVER LINING

The Social Security Administration has given divorced people claiming options, which provides them with opportunities to increase or maximize their Social Security income. If you are divorced, being aware of these options could make a huge difference in substantially increasing your Social Security income and improving your quality of life during your retirement.

If you meet these three qualifications, you could substantially increase the size of your benefit:

1. You must have been married for at least 10 years before you're divorced.

2. You must not be re-married.

3. If you have been divorced for at least two years, your ex-spouse only has to be eligible to receive Social Security benefits.

IMPORTANT NOTICE

With the changes to Social Security resulting from the passage of the Bipartisan Budget Act of 2015, it is unclear if Qualification #3 will still be the rule in all divorce situations. Until they clarify and resolve that situation, all the information and tables in this chapter are based on the assumption that Qualification is still in effect.

A FORMER SPOUSE CAN STILL CLAIM A SPOUSAL BENEFIT AND THE EX-SPOUSE DOES NOT NEED TO KNOW

Normally, the Spousal Benefit is only available to a married couple, but as a divorced spouse, if you meet all the qualifications, you qualify to receive a Spousal Benefit even though you are no longer married. You will be eligible to receive up to 50%, or one-half of the size of your ex-spouse's Full Retirement Age Work History Benefit. Claiming a Spousal Benefit does not change the benefit that your ex-spouse will receive in any way and your ex-spouse does not need to know you are doing it.

CASE STUDY: PAT AND CORY ARE DIVORCED

Depending upon the circumstances, the Spousal Benefit can be used in several different ways. In each of the following examples, it is assumed that Pat and Cory are the same age. In this first situation, I assume that Pat's Work History Benefit at her Full Retirement Age is going to be $500 per month. Cory's Work History Benefit at his Full Retirement Age is $2,000 per month. If the former spouses do not meet the qualifications, Pat will not be able to claim a Spousal Benefit and can only claim her Work History Benefit of $500.

TABLE 14.1

Cory's Full Retirement Age Benefit - $2,000
Pat's Full Retirement Age Benefit - $500

Age	62	63	64	65	66	67	68	69	70
Pat's Monthly Social Security	$0	$0	$0	$0	$500	$500	$500	$500	$500
Pat's Annual Social Security	$0	$0	$0	$0	$6,000	$6,000	$6,000	$6,000	$6,000

Pat can only claim her own Work History Benefit of $500 per month

Table 14.1 shows Pat's monthly and annual Social Security benefits at different ages if she COULD NOT claim a Spousal Benefit. She waits until her Full Retirement Age of 66 and claims her Work History Benefit of $500 per month, receiving $6,000 ($500 x 12) of Social Security income for the year. This is the amount of Social Security income Pat will receive every year for the rest of her life.

PAT CLAIMS A SPOUSAL BENEFIT AT 66

TABLE 14.2

Cory's Full Retirement Age Benefit - $2,000
Pat's Full Retirement Age Benefit - $500

Age	62	63	64	65	66	67	68	69
Pat's Monthly Social Security	$0	$0	$0	$0	$1,000	$1,000	$1,000	$1,000
Pat's Annual Social Security	$0	$0	$0	$0	$12,000	$12,000	$12,000	$12,000

Pat claims a Spousal Benefit at age 66 and receives 50% of Cory's benefit (50% x $2,000 = $1,000)

If the former spouses had been married for at least 10 years before their divorce, Pat, who has not remarried, would be allowed to claim a Spousal

Benefit, significantly changing the amount of her Social Security income. Table 14.2 shows you what Pat's monthly and annual Social Security benefits would be at different ages if she could claim a Spousal Benefit. In this case, the smartest thing for Pat to do is to wait until her Full Retirement Age of 66 and claim a Spousal Benefit. She is entitled to 50% of Cory's Work History Benefit, or 50% of $2,000, which is $1,000 per month. At age 66, Pat starts to receive her benefit of $1,000 per month or $12,000 for the year. She is guaranteed to receive this amount of money for the rest of her life. If Cory dies before she does, her Social Security income will increase yet again.

I did not include any annual COLA adjustments in either Table 14.1 or Table 14.2 because I thought the numbers would be easier to understand without the COLA adjustments. If I had included an annual COLA increase, the numbers in Table 14.2 would have experienced a larger dollar increase each year.

PAT CLAIMS HER BENEFIT AT 62

If Pat does not wait until she is age 66, and claims her Social Security benefits at age 62, she is still better off in the long run because she is eligible for a Spousal Benefit. If she claims her benefits at age 62, depending on the benefit she is qualified to receive either her Work History Benefit, or her Spousal Benefit will be reduced. Her Spousal Benefit will still be substantially higher than her Work History Benefit.

TABLE 14.3

Cory's Full Retirement Age Benefit - $2,000 Pat's Full Retirement Age Benefit - $500									
Age	62	63	64	65	66	67	68	69	70
Pat's Monthly Social Security	$375	$375	$375	$375	$375	$375	$375	$375	$375
Pat's Annual Social Security	$4,500	$4,500	$4,500	$4,500	$4,500	$4,500	$4,500	$4,500	$4,500

In Table 14.3, I have assumed that Pat had been married for less than 10 years before her divorce, so she was not eligible to claim a Spousal Benefit. The only benefit she could claim was her own Work History Benefit, which she claims at age 62. Because she claimed her Work History Benefit four years earlier than her Full Retirement Age (age 66), the benefit was reduced by 25% and the dollar amount she receives starting at age 62 is $375 per month and $4,500 for the year. This is the amount of Social Security income she will receive every year for the rest of her life.

TABLE 14.4

Cory's Full Retirement Age Benefit - $2,000 Pat's Full Retirement Age Benefit - $500									
Age	62	63	64	65	66	67	68	69	70
Pat's Monthly Social Security	$700	$700	$700	$700	$700	$700	$700	$700	$700
Pat's Annual Social Security	$8,400	$8,400	$8,400	$8,400	$8,400	$8,400	$8,400	$8,400	$8,400

In Table 14.4, I assumed that Pat was married for more than 10 years before her divorce and she has never remarried. Therefore, she qualifies for a Spousal Benefit. Because she claimed her benefit early at age 62, it is reduced and she receives a total benefit of 35% of Cory's Full Retirement Age Work History Benefit, or $700 per month ($2,000 x .35). By claiming her benefit at age 62, Pat will receive a monthly Social Security check of $700 per month and $8,400 for the year. She is guaranteed to receive this amount of money for the rest of her life, but if her ex-husband dies before she does, her Social Security income will increase again.

SOCIAL SECURITY MAY GIVE YOU THE UPGRADE TO THE SPOUSAL BENEFIT AUTOMATICALLY

In the previous two examples, Social Security may automatically pay you the higher benefit if you qualify for a Spousal Benefit, and if it is larger than your regular Work History Benefit. When you file or apply for your benefits, Social Security will ask if you were ever divorced and if you were married for more than 10 years before your divorce. If you meet all of their qualifications, and a Spousal Benefit would be larger than your regular Work History Benefit, they will often automatically pay you the larger benefit. If you disclose the information about your divorce when you apply for benefits, Social Security should automatically pay you the higher benefit if you qualify.

MANY DIVORCED SPOUSES CAN STILL USE THE RESTRICTED APPLICATION CLAIMING STRATEGY

If you are a divorced spouse and were age 62 or older before January 1, 2016, you are still qualified to use the Restricted Application claiming strategy. You don't have to use or implement the strategy before that date. If you are age 62 before January 1, 2016, you are "Grandfathered" and can still use the strategy after that date. Don't count on Social Security telling you that you are qualified to use this strategy, chances are you are going to have to ask them for it. Using the Restricted Application strategy could pay you tens of thousands of dollars in additional Social Security income and make it easier for you to maximize the dollar amount of your benefit.

In this example, Pat's Full Retirement Age Work History Benefit is $1,250 per month and Cory's is $2,000 per month. When you first look at this example, you may think that it doesn't make sense for Pat to claim a Spousal Benefit at age 66 because it will only pay her $1,000 per month (50% x $2,000).

Why would she claim a Spousal Benefit and receive only $1,000 per month instead of claiming her own Work History Benefit of $1,250 per month?

TABLE 14.5

Cory's Full Retirement Age Benefit - $2,000
Pat's Full Retirement Age Benefit - $1,250

Age	62	63	64	65	66	67	68	69	70
Pat's Monthly Social Security	$0	$0	$0	$0	($1,250)	$1,250	$1,250	$1,250	$1,250
Pat's Annual Social Security	$0	$0	$0	$0	$15,000	$15,000	$15,000	$15,000	$15,000

Pat claims her own Work History Benefit.

Let's take a look at what appears to be the obvious course of action. In Table 14.5, Pat claims her own Work History Benefit of $1,250 per month at age 66 ($15,000 for the year). She does not even consider claiming a Spousal Benefit at age 66 because the Spousal Benefit will only pay her $1,000 per month. Why would she accept less money every month by claiming a Spousal Benefit?

TABLE 14.6

Cory's Full Retirement Age Benefit - $2,000									
Pat's Full Retirement Age Benefit - $1,250									
Age	62	63	64	65	66	67	68	69	70
Pat's Monthly Social Security	$0	$0	$0	$0	$1,000	$1,000	$1,000	$1,000	$1,650
Pat's Annual Social Security	$0	$0	$0	$0	$12,000	$12,000	$12,000	$12,000	$19,800

Pat claims and restricts her benefit to only a Spousal Benefit	Pat switches to her maxed out Work History Benefit and receives $1,650 for the rest of her life.

In Table 14.6, Pat waits until her Full Retirement Age of 66 to claim any benefits. She restricts her benefit to a Spousal Benefit and receives 50% of her ex-husband's benefit or $1,000 per month ($12,000 for the year). By restricting her benefit to only a Spousal Benefit at age 66, she continues to delay claiming her own Work History Benefit. Every year that she delays claiming her Work History Benefit after age 66, she earns Delayed Retirement Credits of 8% per year, increasing the size of her own Work History Benefit.

PAT SWITCHES TO HER OWN WORK HISTORY BENEFIT AND GETS A BIGGER PAY DAY

In Table 14.6, Pat receives a Spousal Benefit of $1,000 per month for a period of four years while she is 66, 67, 68, and 69 years old. At the end of those four years, when she is 70 years old, the amount of her still-unclaimed Work History Benefit has grown by 32% (8% x 4 years), bringing the total amount up to $1,650 ($1,250 x 132%) per month. At age 70, she switches from the Spousal Benefit of $1,000 per month to her own maxed-out Work History Benefit of $1,650 per month. This is the amount of the check she will receive every month for the rest of her life (unless her ex-husband passes away first, and then her income will increase again).

PAT GETS PAID TO WAIT

Even though, at age 66, she received a smaller check—$1,000 per month instead of $1,250 per month—in the form of a Spousal Benefit, Pat received a check that was only slightly smaller and the situation was temporary, lasting for only four years. In Table 14.5, if Pat claimed her Work History Benefit at age 66, she would have received a Social Security check of $1,250 per month ($15,000 for the year). In Table 14.6, if she claimed a Spousal Benefit at age 66 and switched to her own Work History Benefit four years later, at age 70, she would receive a Social Security check of $1,650 per month ($19,800 for the year). That's almost $5,000 ($19,800 - $15,000) more Social Security income that she will receive every year for the rest of her life. By claiming and restricting her benefit to a Spousal Benefit at age 66, it made it easier for her to maximize the size of her own Work History Benefit at age 70, which also greatly increased the amount of Social Security income she will receive over her retirement lifetime. The inclusion of COLA adjustments would make the benefit even larger over time.

THREE KEY FACTORS ARE REQUIRED TO MAKE THIS APPROACH WORK:

• You must be age 62 or older before January 1, 2016.

• In order to be able to switch from a Spousal Benefit to a higher Work History Benefit at a later age, the Spousal Benefit must be claimed at your Full Retirement Age or later.

• If you want to claim only a Spousal Benefit at your Full Retirement Age (66) and switch to your higher Work History Benefit at a later age (age 70, for example), then, when you claim your Spousal Benefit at age 66, you must notify the Social Security Administration that you want to RESTRICT YOUR BENEFIT TO ONLY A SPOUSAL BENEFIT. If you do not notify them to RESTRICT YOUR BENEFIT TO ONLY A SPOUSAL BENEFIT, they will assume you are claiming your own Work History Benefit at age 66.

THE EX-HUSBAND CAN DO IT TOO!

In all of these examples, it was assumed that the ex-wife was the lower-earning spouse with the smaller Social Security Benefit. However, if the ex-husband is the lower-earning spouse with the smaller Social Security benefit, he can take advantage of the Spousal Benefit in the same way to maximize his Social Security benefits.

IT'S NOT JUST FOR THE EX-SPOUSE WITH THE SMALLER BENEFIT

The ex-spouse with the higher benefit can also use a Spousal Benefit to help maximize his or her Social Security Benefits. Look back at the example above where Pat's benefit, at her Full Retirement Age, was $1,250 per month and Cory's was $2,000 per month. Even though Cory has the larger Social Security benefit, he can use the Spousal Benefit to help maximize his Social Security income.

CORY MAXIMIZES HIS INCOME USING THE SPOUSAL BENEFIT

If Cory's goal is to maximize the size of his Social Security check, he can do that if he waits until he is age 70 to claim his Work History Benefit. Waiting until age 70 to claim his Work History Benefit does not mean he has to wait that long before he receives any Social Security income.

TABLE 14.7

Cory's Full Retirement Age Benefit - $2,000
Pat's Full Retirement Age Benefit - $1,250

Age	62	63	64	65	66	67	68	69	70
Cory's Monthly Social Security	$0	$0	$0	$0	$625	$625	$625	$625	$2,640
Cory's Annual Social Security	$0	$0	$0	$0	$7,500	$7,500	$7,500	$7,500	$31,680

Cory claims and restricts his benefit to only a Spousal Benefit and receives $625 per month

Cory switches to his own maxed out Work History Benefit and receives $2,640 per month for the rest of his life

Cory can use the Spousal Benefit to make it easier to maximize his Social Security benefits. In Table 14.7, at age 66, Cory can claim and restrict his benefit to a Spousal Benefit and receive 50% of Pat's Work History Benefit. Pat's Work History Benefit, at her Full Retirement Age, is $1,250; half of that is $625 per month. At age 66, Cory can receive a Spousal Benefit of $625 per month ($7,500 per year). He can collect that Spousal Benefit over the next four years at ages 66, 67, 68, and 69. Over that four-year period, his still-unclaimed Work History Benefit continues to earn Delayed Retirement Credits, growing by 8% every year. At age 70, Cory switches from the Spousal Benefit to his maxed-out Work History Benefit, which has grown to $2,640 per month ($31,680 for the year). Collecting the Spousal Benefit for that four-year period of time made it easier for Cory to delay claiming his own Work History Benefit until age 70.

RUN YOUR NUMBERS IN MY ON-LINE CALCULATOR—WWW.GETTINGPAIDTOWAIT.COM

> If you would like to see if you could use the Spousal Benefit to increase your Social Security income, go to my website at www. GettingPaidToWait.com and input your own Social Security benefit numbers into the Social Security Calculator. Customized results will be generated in a matter of a few seconds based on the concepts in this book. The Social Security claiming strategy that best suits your personal situation and maximizes your benefits will be suggested.

SURVIVOR BENEFIT RULES FOR DIVORCED SPOUSES

Every divorced spouse should be aware of the Survivor Benefit rules, especially if you are the ex-spouse receiving the smaller Social Security Benefit. The larger the Survivor Benefit, the better it is for the surviving spouse. The Survivor Benefit can play a big role in the life of the divorced spouse who receives the smaller Social Security benefit.

HERE'S HOW IT WORKS:

The qualifications for an ex-spouse claiming a Survivor Benefit are the same as claiming a Spousal Benefit, with one exception—you cannot be remarried if you are younger than age 60. However, if you wait until at least age 60 to remarry, you will still be eligible to claim a Survivor Benefit based on the Work History Benefit of your former spouse.

PAT TAKES ADVANTAGE OF CORY'S SURVIVOR BENEFIT

TABLE 14.8

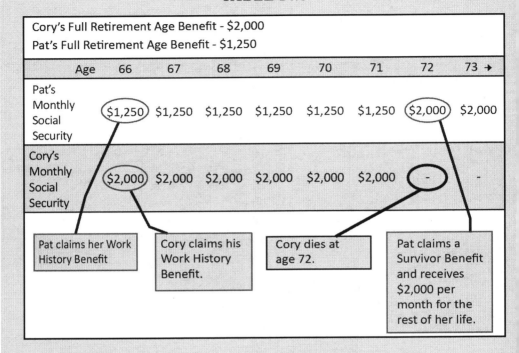

Cory's Full Retirement Age Benefit - $2,000							
Pat's Full Retirement Age Benefit - $1,250							
Age 66	67	68	69	70	71	72	73 →
Pat's Monthly Social Security $1,250	$1,250	$1,250	$1,250	$1,250	$1,250	$2,000	$2,000
Cory's Monthly Social Security $2,000	$2,000	$2,000	$2,000	$2,000	$2,000	-	-

Pat claims her Work History Benefit

Cory claims his Work History Benefit.

Cory dies at age 72.

Pat claims a Survivor Benefit and receives $2,000 per month for the rest of her life.

Let's look at the case where Pat's benefit, at her Full Retirement Age, is $1,250 per month and Cory's benefit is $2,000 per month. Assuming they are both the same age, in Table 14.2, Pat claims her Full Retirement Age benefit of $1,250 at age 66 and Cory claims his Full Retirement Age benefit of $2,000 also at age 66. If Cory passes away at age 72, Pat can claim a Survivor Benefit and begin receiving the entire amount of Cory's regular monthly benefit of $2,000 per month.

THE NEW SPOUSE AND THE FORMER SPOUSE CAN TAKE ADVANTAGE OF THE SPOUSAL BENEFIT AND THE SURVIVOR BENEFIT

What happens if the ex-spouse with the larger Social Security benefit remarries? Does this affect the other ex-spouse's ability to claim either a

Spousal Benefit or a Survivor Benefit? The answer is no, it does not affect the ex-spouse's ability to claim either a Spousal Benefit or a Survivor Benefit. If we assume that Cory had remarried, then both his current wife and Pat would be eligible to receive a Survivor Benefit. In our last example, when Cory dies, both Pat and his current wife would be able to claim a Survivor Benefit of $2,000 per month. They would each receive $2,000 per month from Social Security for the rest of their lives. In fact, if Cory had been divorced twice and remarried again for the third time, all three of them, his two ex-wives (as long as they met the qualifications) and his current wife, would be able to receive a Survivor Benefit check from Social Security of $2,000 per month. It works the same way for the Spousal Benefit as well.

IF YOUR FORMER SPOUSE HAS DIED, IT'S STILL NOT TOO LATE

If you have an ex-spouse that has died and their Social Security benefit was larger than yours, you can still claim a Survivor Benefit. Claiming a Survivor Benefit will entitle you to receive the same size check that your ex-spouse received when he or she was alive. Even if your ex-spouse died many years ago, and you did not claim a Survivor Benefit at the time of his or her death, you can still claim it now and start to receive that larger check moving forward. You just have to inform your local Social Security office. They may ask you for proof that you were married to your now-deceased ex-spouse for at least 10 years prior to your divorce and did not remarry before age 60. Once you provide that information, they should immediately start sending you the larger Survivor Benefit check. The same would be true for the Spousal Benefit, except, in order to claim a Spousal Benefit based on your ex-spouse's Work History Benefit, you can't be remarried at any age.

TELL YOUR DIVORCED FRIENDS

The majority of divorced people in this country are not aware that these Social Security options are available to them. Both qualified divorced spouses can take advantage of these options. Regardless of whether you are the ex-spouse with the smaller benefit, or the ex-spouse with the larger benefit, you need to be aware of these options because they can help to substantially increase your Social Security income and greatly improve your quality of life during your retirement.

CHAPTER 14 IMPORTANT CONCEPTS:

• The Social Security Administration has given divorced people, who were married for at least 10 years before their divorce, claiming options that can make it even easier for them to increase their Social Security income.

• Divorced spouses, who meet all of the qualifications, are entitled to claim a Spousal Benefit or Survivor Benefit based on the Work History Benefit of their ex-spouse.

• Claiming a Spousal Benefit does not change the benefit that your ex-spouse will receive in any way.

• Claiming a Survivor Benefit will entitle you to receive the same size check that your ex-spouse received when he or she was alive.

SOURCES:

1. Brown, Susan and Lin, I-Fen, The Gray Divorce Revolution: Rising Divorce Among Middle-aged and Older Adults, 1990–2010 (United States: National Center for Family & Marriage Research, August 2012)

2. Social Security Administration, The Retirement Prospects of Divorced Women (United States: SSA November 1, 2012)

SOME FINAL WORDS

Congratulations! Now that you have read this book, you know more about our Social Security system and how to maximize your benefits than the vast majority of people in this country. You also know that if you are age 66 or older before May 1, 2016 you are still eligible to use the File and Suspend claiming Strategy, and most importantly, you have to use or implement that strategy before that date. Now you know that if you are age 62 or older before January 1, 2016, you are still eligible to use the Claim Early, Claim Late (Restricted Application) strategy but you DO NOT have to implement the strategy before that date.

Using either of these strategies could pay you tens of thousands of dollars in additional Social Security income and make it easier for you to maximize the size of your benefits. Before you claim your Social Security benefits you need to first find out if you are qualified to use either one of these claiming strategies and how they would work in your personal situation. One of the best ways to find that out is by visiting my website, www.gettingpaidtowait. com, and using my Paid to Wait Social Security calculator. It will tell you if you are qualified to use either or both strategies and exactly how they would work in your situation.

GOOD LUCK WITH YOUR CLAIMING DECISION.

ABOUT THE AUTHOR

Brian Doherty's career began as a financial advisor and throughout his 30 years in the financial services industry, he has held various senior management positions. He was President and CEO of Key Bank's investment subsidiary, Key Investments, and Vice President and National Sales Manager for New York Life's Retirement Income Security division.

Presently, Mr. Doherty is President of Filtech, a consulting company specializing in Social Security claiming strategies, which helps retirees maximize their Social Security benefits. He has been a featured speaker for many of the largest financial institutions in the country. Mr. Doherty graduated from Syracuse University with a MBA in Finance and received his BS in Accounting from Elmira College.